THE COLLECTOR'S GUIDE
QUINTESSENTIALLY
GEMS

THE COLLECTOR'S GUIDE
QUINTESSENTIALLY GEMS

QUINTESSENTIALLY
PUBLISHING

ALEXANDRA MOR ✦ BOUCHERON
BUCCELLATI ✦ BVLGARI ✦ CARNET
CARTIER ✦ CHOPARD ✦ CINDY CHAO
YEWN ✦ FABERGÉ
FABIO SALINI ✦ FARAH KHAN
FRANCIS MERTENS ✦ GEMFIELDS ✦ JAR
JJBUCKAR ✦ LENA SKLYUT ✦ LEVIEV
LORENZ BÄUMER ✦ MARGHERITA BURGENER
MICHAEL YOUSSOUFIAN ✦ MIKIMOTO PEARLS
MING ✦ NADA G ✦ NICHOLAS VARNEY ✦ OCTIUM
POONAM SONI ✦ SARAH HO ✦ SHARON KHAZZAM
SHAWISH ✦ THEO FENNELL
VAN CLEEF&ARPELS ✦ YVES FREY
VICENTE GRACIA ✦ WALLACE CHAN
WENDY YUE ✦ ZOLTAN DAVID

CONTENTS

For further information on images go to Index page 204_211

INTRODUCTION BY TAMARA KAMINSKY

As with so many great adventures, my foray into the luminous world of Fine Jewellery and Gems began in conversation with a stranger in a café. It was Milan in the late 90s when mainstream jewellery houses were happily producing solitaire diamonds on platinum chains for the masses and cult jewellery, and when collectors' pieces enjoyed an underground status amongst the appreciative few. My knowledge of jewels came through advertising and marketing campaigns, which rarely do justice either to the wealth of work out there or to the skills and fascinating processes which bring these magnificent pieces to life. I did, however, have an eye for Italian style and the woman sitting next to me in all her Italian splendour was casually dressed in ripped jeans and t-shirt, platform leather boots, a designer handbag and a short swing chinchilla fur coat.

Newly dispatched from high school, I was captivated by her casual and unpretentious attitude toward luxury. She shot back her espresso and turned to leave, only to catch me peering curiously at her. Purely through awkwardness, I pointed towards two barely visible gold earrings, hidden almost entirely by a mass of shiny black curls and mumbled a compliment. Within seconds, her icy exterior had melted and she had slid onto a bar stool next to me, unhooking her earrings, holding them to the light and inviting me to hold them. They were by an artist jeweller called Ted Muehling. I have since collected a few pieces of his, although not particularly expensive ones. Every time I hold them or feel them I can smell the aroma of fresh Italian espresso and feel the chill of an early winter in Northern Italy.

This is the magic of a collector. They are by far the greatest advocate any jeweller can have. As with any collector, it is not merely the objects they love. It is the process of learning about them, refining their tastes and also their eye for the best of what is out there. In the case of Fine Jewellery collectors, they must also share a passion for collecting with the designers themselves. After all, a jeweller will collect stones, ideas and settings. It is up to them where they choose to use these precious gifts and who they choose to gift them to.

Within this work I have focused largely on independent fine jewellers, simply because their clientele is smaller and they are known only by and to collectors and nobody else. Also represented, albeit perhaps too briefly, are the larger houses of Van Cleef & Arpels, Cartier, Chopard, Bulgari and Boucheron. This is because they have such a magnificent selection of their own books that it seems superfluous for me to add a great deal to their story.

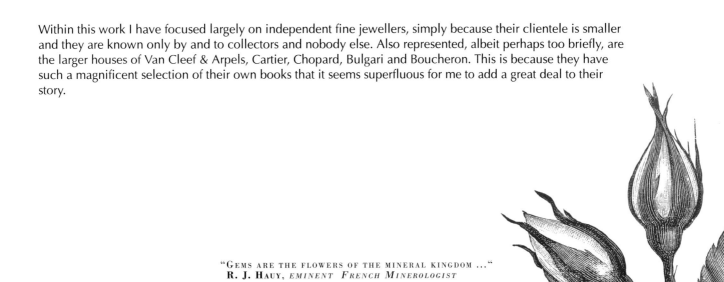

"GEMS ARE THE FLOWERS OF THE MINERAL KINGDOM ..."
R. J. HAUY, *EMINENT FRENCH MINEROLOGIST*

GEM: A PRECIOUS STONE CUT AND POLISHED FOR ORNAMENT;
      a: SOMETHING PRIZED ESPECIALLY FOR GREAT BEAUTY OR
          PERFECTION
      b: A PERFECTLY FORMED AND ROBUST FLOWER BUD

JAR

"EVERYTHING CONSPIRES TO MAKE YOU...MORE PUBLIC...MY PASSION FOR HAPPINESS TOLD ME TO STAY SMALL, STAY SILENT."

JOEL ARTHUR ROSENTHAL

If there is a single living jeweller on the planet, to whom all other jewellers will happily play second fiddle, it is Parisian jeweller Joel Arthur Rosenthal. Rosenthal, the man, is a mystery. He does not partake in publicity, nor does he allow images of his new pieces to be seen in any publications, nor, indeed in the windows of his showroom in Paris. In fact, he does not have windows in his showroom. Even the door handle for this secret spot is difficult to find. So unique and beautifully crafted and distinctive are his pieces, that following an exhibition in London in 2002 the hardback book which accompanied the works became auction-worthy in itself. The luxury of owning photographic renderings of JAR pieces is now so rare that it commands a higher price than a diamond and platinum ring from Tiffany's Jewellers. So what is it that makes JAR the most exclusive jeweller in the world? The fact that you need to be invited to gain access to his studio to look at his work and to have the opportunity to purchase one of his pieces is one reason. Another is the fact that only those with a keen eye for the

jeweller's craft can see what makes the pieces stand out from all others and that only a tight selection of jewellery collectors in the world meets all of these requirements.
JAR sets the standard not just for Fine Jewellery, but for Fine Jewellery collectors as well.

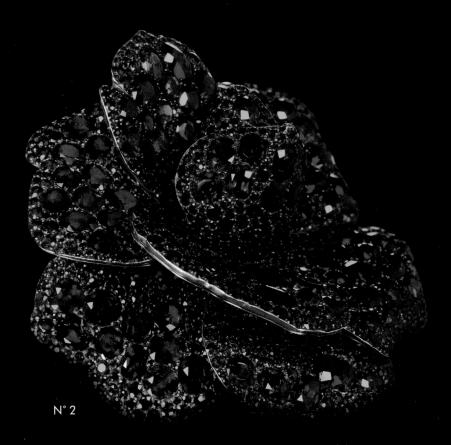

N° 2

THE COLLECTOR

Dreams & Aspirations

THE COLLECTOR

BY TAMARA KAMINSKY

"There are many people aspiring to have a piece of history or a jewel worthy of a museum collection. As a serious collector, one must arrive before the pack, which with jewellery means either exploring quality unsigned pieces or newly crafted works of art made by the finest designers and craftsmen."

Suzanne Tennenbaum / collector of Van Cleef & Arpels and author

The clear measure of a jewellery collector's eminence is the tension in an auction room as one of their jewels goes under the hammer. Their lives, be they outrageous, scandalous or simply glamorous are engrained in the jewel forever, making it far more valuable than the sum of its parts. Curators, collectors, the rich and the powerful are left to decide amongst themselves just how esteemed the late owner was.

When an entire collection is open for bidding, a small frenzy ensues not just amongst jewellery collectors, but also the general public. The 2012 auction of Elizabeth Taylor's jewels reached epic proportions. With an international tour of the collection pulling in crowds from all walks of life queuing to see this immaculate assortment of precious pieces, the late Dame Taylor garnered more attention than she had for decades as a living Hollywood A-Lister. It was not all hype. The prices gleaned from the sale amazed even their auctioneers, who had

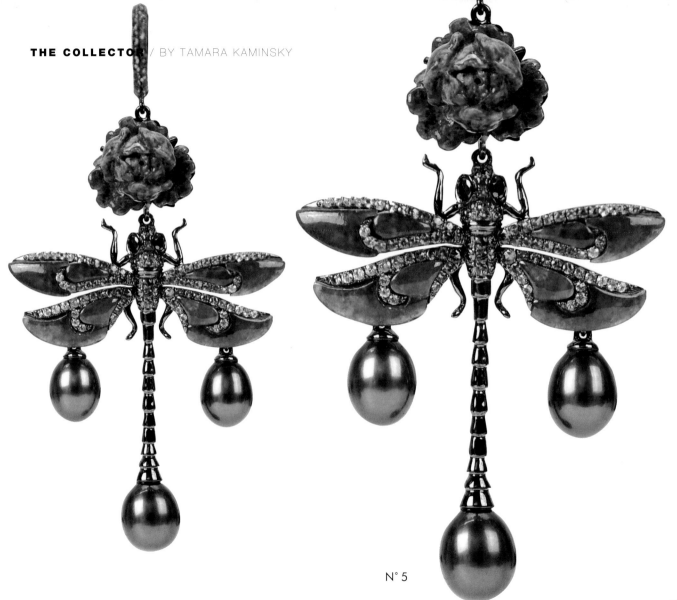

N° 5

N° 6

grossly underestimated the actress' popularity. The star, somewhat tarnished at the end of her life, re-emerged in the glimmering light of these gems, glowing as she did when she was first launched by her Hollywood studio as a teenager.

Her jewels have not merely left her immortalised, but restored her to her youth. A fine sign-off for the great star, who would have been thrilled with such a eulogy. Always one to have the last word, Taylor would have been particularly amused by the attention paid to her jewels by other serious jewellery collectors. Painfully aware of her own vulgarity in the eyes of those in high society, (especially because of her love of giant stones), the fact that those same detractors were now desperately bidding to own such pieces would have filled her with wicked glee.

Taylor is not the only collector to have her jewels auctioned off within a year of her passing. A cynic would chalk things down to it being a matter of settling the departed's great estate. Although this is undeniable, these curated auctions with their beautifully printed catalogues and visitors travelling far and wide for viewings and to hear the stories behind

the collections, is surely the most personal and fitting tribute for anyone who loved jewellery.

The notorious Wallis Simpson was such a person. Two substantially important jewellery collections to hit the auction block were both from the late Simpson, famous on both sides of the Atlantic for seducing her lover, Edward VIII into abdicating from the British throne. Controversy, scandal, elegance and American bravura surround The Duchess of Windsor even post-humously. Her fabulous life made her an icon and the beauty of her jewels and magnificent style became her lasting legacy. Wallis did what every serious collector aims to do: she became an integral part of the story of jewellery and challenge the artists to take their work to the next level.

The best example of this would be Wallis' commission for Van Cleef & Arpels in the 1930s. Looking for a platinum and diamond zipper for a gown she particularly loved, she approached the Maison believing in their technical ability. She was right but she vastly underestimated the task at hand. It took the craftsmen until 1951 to produce what is still their greatest achievement. Unzipped, it is a

N° 7

necklace, and when zipped, a bracelet. This design is reinterpreted regularly by the house and each piece becomes another collector's item. A collector who was not afraid to throw down the gauntlet, was The Maharajah of Patiala who famously approached Boucheron with six chests bursting with gems and who asked for one of the largest known commissions in the history of jewellery. This would have pushed the already imaginative jeweller to another level, in production volume alone. It would also have given him tremendous freedom to create pieces with no limits.

Such collectors still abound. The difference between a collector and someone who just loves to purchase beautiful things lies in their knowledge of jewels and also their selective taste. Suzanne Tennenbaum not only collects Van Cleef&Arpels jewellery but she is so knowledgeable on the subject that she was able to write about their work.

Favouring pieces from the Deco period and the 1930s, she is of course, "fascinated by the zipper necklace". This is not simply for its beauty but for "its innovation and the fact that it can actually zip closed, to convert into a bracelet." Tennenbaum also understands the other technical achievements of the Parisian jeweller, having first purchased one of their mystery set brooches, before becoming a more avid collector. She explains, "I appreciated the Ludo

N° 8

N° 9

bracelets with sliding ball closures as well as the passe-partout. These jewels incorporate functional elements with exceptional design".

Whereas most high jewellery purchases are cloaked in secrecy, some ladies are happy to part from their jewels for the right reason. Ellen Barkin, in 2006 sold off the jewels her husband had bought her throughout their marriage, after her divorce was finalised. A perfect way to turn over a new leaf and she instantly became known worldwide for her immeasurable taste as a collector and as a serious patron of some of the greatest living jewellers.

In particular, the jewels of Joel Arthur Rosenthal took centre stage in the auction; not least because it is the only opportunity most people will ever get to seeing or purchasing one in person. JAR of Paris selects his clients carefully, placing Barkin with her generous collection, firmly in the history books as a collector of note.

A few years later, she was followed by Lily Safra, who sold her collection off for charity. Another JAR collector, her name will be as synonymous with taste

as it will with philanthropy. Due in many ways to such women, the art of jewellery collection has become a high-brow, serious exercise, not merely a question of liberally spending and amassing the largest and most expensive jewels on the market. The editing of a collection has become the most important aspect of serious patronage.

Even more importantly, discovering new artists, gaining exclusive access to them and inspiring them are what the time-honoured ritual of collecting fine jewellery is all about.

THE
DYNASTIES

The Dynasties

BOUCHERON

"TO ME, BOUCHERON IS THE VANGUARD
OF ART JEWELLERY."

SHAUN LEANE, JEWELLER

The jewels of Boucheron are as seductive as the women who have bought and collected them over the ages. Amongst them, the notorious and supremely glamorous courtesan, Marquise de Païva was a regular customer of Boucheron, purchasing, amongst other things, a brooch with a 100 ct yellow diamond in the centre. The Countess of Castiglione, Virginia Oldoni, mistress to Napoleon III, was also a loyal customer of the jeweller, purchasing some ostentatious pieces from the *Maison* over the years. So loyal was she, that when the eccentric secluded herself in later years to hide her withered beauty, she chose a blackened apartment directly over Boucheron's shop on the Place Vendôme. Almost entombed above the jewels, she only ever stepped out at night and banished mirrors from her home. The boutique was purchased by Boucheron in 1893, on the corner of the street, where the light was optimal, so that the jewels in the window would sparkle all the more brightly in the sun. The jewellery had already caught

N° 10

the attention of the public, winning awards at the *Exposition Universelle* as early as 1867, where they won the first of many awards over the years.

The artist jeweller and collaborator Paul Legrand worked at the *Maison* to create some of their most important signature pieces. In particular, the *Question Mark* necklace which wraps around the neck, without the need for a clasp or fastening. In the shape of a flower, a feather or the famous Boucheron serpent, this is still a recurring theme at Boucheron.

N° 11

BUCCELLATI

"I BELIEVE MORE IN THE FUTURE THAN THE PAST."

GIANMARIA BUCCELLATI

The Renaissance is often lauded as The *Golden Age*. So it makes sense that the most celebrated goldsmith in Italy would be inspired by Renaissance craftsmanship and metal work. This is far from a mere stylistic reference however. These are not Renaissance revival pieces, nor historicist replicas. Rather, Buccellati has adopted the highly complex production techniques of that age and finessed them to suit a contemporary collector. The effect is magical. Even the basic gold bands wrap lightly round the finger like lace embroidered with golden threads, like something from a fairy tale. Cuffs have a distinct look in solid gold, with a surface which mimics silk shantung, glittering as it catches the light from all directions. Drop earrings are almost invisible at certain angles as the lattice work is so thin that viewed from the front barely any surface

N° 12

metal can be seen at all. A slight breeze,
however, and the piece will rotate to
become fully visible in all its golden glory;
a web of precious metals, fine gold and
platinum layered and soldered together
by hands that only work in a Buccellati
workshop.

Buccellati pieces are distinguishable
simply because they are the only
remaining house to perform these miracles
with precious metals. No other jeweller
has the experience or the heritage for such
a collection of original designs. All the
Buccellati goldsmiths have been trained
from the age of 14, perfecting their art until
they have risen in the ranks to take on the
responsibility of creating their own pieces
from scratch. Buccellati, himself has been
through this process.

He continues to sketch each creation
by hand, in an instructive goldsmith's

N° 13

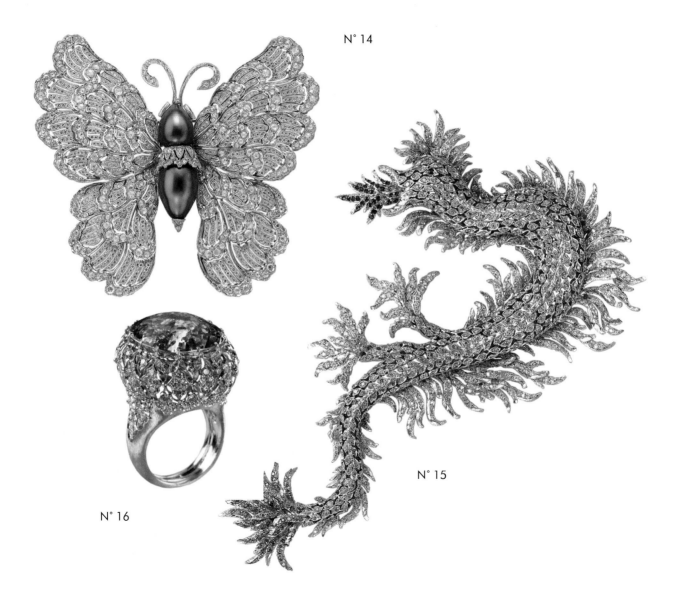

N° 14

N° 15

N° 16

rendering. It is then passed onto his masters, who will begin the multi-layered process which will become a Buccellati masterpiece. An avid collector himself, Mario has a love of natural baroque pearls, around which he has created a collection of jewels.

These are especially important to Buccellati's international collectors as they are, in a sense, a joint collection between his clients and himself. Each pearl has been kept lovingly by the designer who only lets them go out of love and trust for the women who wish to wear a unique Buccellati heirloom. By wearing one of his pearl creations, his collectors become a part of the Buccellati family. The same,

of course, could be said for any one of the masterpieces that this unique jewellery house has sold in the past century. In particular, their magnificent neckpieces, made from a honeycomb textured gold lattice. Each segment is small enough to behave like a single link in a chain. Despite the detail of the gold sections, they fall on the neck like a lace scarf, interrupted only by Briolette set gems within the piece.

These signature Buccellati masterpieces are so light in their design that they have an almost futuristic feel. The answers lie in the techniques of the Renaissance and the vision of Mario Buccellati. The *Golden Age* lives on…

BVLGARI

If *La Dolce Vita* could be harnessed in a jewel, that jewel would be emblazoned with the Bulgari logo. Luscious, large as life and brimming with sensuality and Mediterranean warmth, this is the brand which brought unabashed luxury to Italy's capital. Arriving in Rome from his native Greece in 1881, Sotirio Bulgari soon transferred his skills as a silversmith to creating fine jewellery in the discipline of the French goldsmith school, as every Haute Jeweller felt compelled to do. The boutique helped to garner the brand's reputation for quality production of beautiful platinum and diamond pieces, bringing Parisian chic to Italy. However, it was only after the Second World War that this house really came into its own. Bulgari's two sons created the signature all Italian look, fresh with the Greco-Roman Classicism influences true to the family's heritage that the brand is known for to this day. The

N° 18

voluminous yellow gold pieces echoed the sleek, soft and rounded aesthetic that Italian design is still celebrated for.

A striking departure from the sharp, serious, all diamond sputnik inspired jewels that were monopolising the jewellery world in the Fifties, Bulgari's pieces exploded with colour and buoyancy. Their use of multiple large cabochon stones, in a myriad of colours further cemented the Bulgari's belief that ostentatious luxury could also be fashionable and fun. A new generation of collectors emerged, bored of their mother's staid pearls and diamonds, to invest in serious jewellery that could be worn everyday without restraint.

CARTIER

"JOAILLIER DES ROIS, ROI DES JOAILLIERS."

King Edward VII

The name Cartier is probably the most famous name in Fine Jewellery today. The company is named after its founder, Louis-François Cartier but it was his three grandsons, Louis, Pierre and Jacques, who made the *Maison* the new benchmark jewellery in style, innovation and design. The *Tutti Frutti* design was inspired by carved gems the brothers brought back from India. Their exotic and playful multi-coloured palette became a staple for the house and the *Tutti Frutti* jewel is still reinterpreted for current collectors. Throughout the jazz age, Cartier presented platinum jewels to a new generation of independent women. The long *sautoir* necklaces in white lustrous metal were often decorated with polished black onyx, diamonds and other carved exotic coloured stones. A heavy pendant or tassel would often finish the design, giving the jewel enough weight to hang properly.

In this period the Cartier *Panthère* was born. An exotic predator with seductive green eyes and supreme elegance, the cat soon became emblematic of the house, and was later made

N° 20

famous by the Duchess of Windsor, one of Cartier's greatest collectors.

A daring woman, she also wore two silver Cartier cuffs, decorated with gold spheres, inspired by the machine age, which ushered in the *Art Moderne* movement. Only a jeweller of this calibre would have the audacity to create fine jewellery from silver. This is what keeps the house of Cartier on the cutting edge of style.

N° 21

CHOPARD

"THERE IS DEFINITELY A BOND BETWEEN FILMS AND JEWELLERY:
A WORLD OF DREAMS."

CAROLINE SCHEUFELE

Every gown in the world has a Chopard jewel to compliment it. Be it a classic black dress, a red carpet knock out gown or a piece of Vintage Couture, this family owned Haute Jeweller creates such a variety of eye-catching pieces that they are a one-stop shop for screen actresses who want to look their optimal on the red carpet. Promising unparalleled luxury, Chopard's high jewellery collections focus on the woman wearing the jewels, in addition to bedazzled onlookers. Their jewels are not just exquisite in a casement window, under lights. They also flatter and beautify women; cascading diamond earrings fall just so, to elongate the neck, a gems set sautoir necklace balances delicately on the collar bone, catching the light; a latticework bracelet gathers around the wrist. These jewels make glamour look effortless. The secret lies in the production of the creations, where the same technical mastery and precision is used in high jewellery as with the brand's celebrated timepieces.

N° 22

Outstanding examples of their creative scope and attention to detail are highlighted in their annual red carpet collections. An historical landmark for the brand was the production of their *Animal Kingdom* collection, featuring 150 precious masterpieces, each one an animated scene stolen from nature. In a single neckpiece, three clownfish swim through a fluid fresco of gems, bubbling like cascading water. This opulent mosaic took 750 hours to complete and is composed of 2160 stones. A true collector's dream.

N° 23

FABERGÉ

"THE FABERGÉ FAMILY SHARE THEIR RICH MEMORIES AND STORIES THAT INSPIRE OUR CREATIONS."

KATHARINA FLOHR

The *Belle Époque* was an elaborate stage set for artists of all genres. A close knit circle of creative giants, including Leon Bakst, Coco Chanel, Picasso and Diaghilev played major parts, as well as the great artist-jeweller and goldsmith to the Russian Imperial Court, Peter Carl Fabergé. During Fabergé's lifetime, his sumptuous jewels were the hallmark of women of taste in high society - namely the Tsarina who owned a Fabergé necklace worth £20m in today's money, and Matilda Kshesinskaya a renowned beauty and lover of Tsar Nicholas II, who wore Fabergé's creations on one of her costumes. This was a magnificent sapphire suite, sewn into the fabric of her garment. The collaboration between Fabergé, his patrons, artists and his public had reached its *apogee*. Seized by the Bolsheviks, most of these pieces were lost with the age, illustrating the annals of history. Until another chapter of Fabergé's rich history unfolds. Mysteriously, flashes of his genius were revealed in the discovery of two old candy tins, hidden away in a

N° 24

mansion in St. Petersburg, containing Fabergé jewels to rival anything in any collection around the world. In particular, diamonds and sapphires set invisibly onto a flexible elongated eclipse of gold. Previously, invisible settings were understood to have been invented only half a century later in Paris.

It is this innovative spirit which Katharina Flohr, Fabergé's Creative and Managing Director, is incorporating as the kernel of the Fabergé renaissance.

N° 25

N° 26

N° 27

N° 28

One breathtaking masterpiece is a modern interpretation of one of Fabergé's earlier designs. The *Romanov* Necklace is set with 2,225 gemstones, totalling over 363 carats of diamonds and emeralds. But it is the technical mastery of the piece which has the Fabergé stamp on it. Taking 18 months to create, the greatest living craftsmen struggled to find a way to physically create the piece to Fabergé's instructions.

The famous Fabergé eggs have also been reinterpreted for the contemporary client: women who are looking for beautiful jewels to wear, not simply to own. The bejeweled grandeur of the Romanov Tsars inspired the multi-coloured *Empereur* interpretations of the appealing *Matelassé* quilted egg pendants in *Les Favorites de Fabergé*. Here the sumptuous rose gold quilted cushions are studded with a variety of coloured gems, rubies, amethysts,

orange, yellow, pink and blue sapphires, tsavorite garnets, emeralds, brown and white diamonds. This piece is set in 18 carat rose gold and the pendant is 18mm in height.

The Fabergé High Jewellery collections continue to impress with the dramatic palette of their precious stones; deep red rubies, sapphires and emeralds set against white diamonds and pearls. The jewels echo the richness of the Fabergé Heritage whilst giving the jewels a distinctly modern feel, with organic, voluminous shapes and micro pavé gems occasionally even set into oxidised gold, creating a dark romanticism throughout the collection. Boutiques in New York, London, Geneva and Hong Kong as well as online, offer a taste of Fabergé magic worldwide.

VAN CLEEF & ARPELS

"THESE JEWELS INCORPORATE FUNCTIONAL ELEMENTS WITH EXCEPTIONAL DESIGN."

SUZANNE TENNENBAUM, COLLECTOR AND AUTHOR

The undisputed home of *Haute Joaillerie* is located in Paris' glorious Place Vendôme. Van Cleef & Arpels opened their first boutique there as early as 1906. Celebrated for elegant and refined High Jewellery, Van Cleef & Arpels' exquisite jewels feature rare gems and exceptional settings which are as important to the history and development of fine jewellery over the ages, as they are beloved by those who collect them. In 1926 Renée Puissant the daughter of Van Cleef & Arpels' founding couple

Alfred Van Cleef and Estelle Arpels, became Creative Director and a visionary for the House. During this first half of the century, it developed new expertise and creations that would become real signatures: an ingenious clutch bag made in gold and gemstones called the *Minaudière*, and the convertible jewel *passe-partout*. The impact these pieces had on the Art Deco landscape is unique, showing off what could be achieved in diamonds and precious metals, celebrating the intricate curves and graphic

aesthetic of the movement. Avant-garde techniques and craftsmanship are at the core of Van Cleef & Arpels creations. In particular, pieces featuring the iconic *Mystery Setting* in which stones are set without any visible metal surrounds, are highly desirable to museums and private collectors, and still play a significant role in Van Cleef & Arpels collections today. The gems appear to be magically encased within the design; vibrant red rubies encrusting a delicately beautiful flower. It could only be a creation from the House of Van Cleef & Arpels.

MODERN
CLASSICS

Modern Classics

ALEXANDRA MOR

"WHEN I FIRST SAW PIECES OF THE COLLECTION, I WAS FLOORED. I WAS WOWED...THE CUSTOMER SERVICE IS IMPECCABLE."

AMANDA BROTMAN DESIGNER/FOUNDER OF AMANDA PEARL. COLLECTOR

The elegant drama of these graphic, sweeping lines are Alexandra Mor's tribute to Parisian Deco; a fitting point of reference for a talented designer with a penchant for French Haute Jewellery and demands this same tradition of craftsmanship for her own collections. Her mission is to create for her clients 'heirlooms in the making'. The intricate perfection of one millimetre diamond melee wires with knife-edge detailing are a standard framework found in any signature Alexandra Mor piece. Herculean stones, such as an 85 carat Green Emerald, a 65.89 carat rectangular Rutilated Quartz or lastly a pair of 74.38 carat oval sapphire slices perch on these slender frames, in a gold pronged setting, giving the impression that the gems are floating on the body freely. It is this interplay with proportions which makes this New York based designer's work so memorable. Despite the jewels' traditional leanings, they always spark a curiosity; a need to view them from several angles, if only to see how they are held together. Curiosity is rewarded, as there are always surprises in store. Perhaps it is the deliberate asymmetry of

N° 34

the centre stone, or a pair of 1.4 carat Trapezoid Diamonds flanking it at its base, almost out of sight, which seem to make the pieces evolve at every turn.

Even inside the band of a ring, known only to its wearer, is an internal yellow gold band forged with the AM signature. Despite her bold aesthetic, this designer loves to collaborate with her collectors to design the object of their dreams. Unsurprisingly, they are largely self purchasing women, who buy jewels for themselves and wear them for nobody else.

N° 35

N° 36

FARAH KHAN

"I BELIEVE THAT JEWELLERY SHOULD MAKE YOU FEEL LIKE A PRINCESS WHEN YOU WEAR IT."

FARAH KHAN

For the finest gems, the purest gold and one of the oldest jewellery industries in the world, collectors know to go to India. Yet, when Farah Khan left home to accompany a friend in LA to do a course in Gemology at the renowned Gemological Institute of America, she knew nothing about precious stones. Already artistically minded with a passion for filling sketchbooks with beautiful drawings of anything which inspired her, she naturally saw the gems outside an academic light. The result was a collection of jewellery designs. Sketches from life are still the first phase of all her designs, which are collected by her clients along with the jewellery itself. These studies betray her creative process. A flick through one of these sketchbooks shows the transformation of a tree trunk, an animal, a dancer or gymnast into a finished jewel. It is the form, the rhythm and the colours of scenes from her day to day life which move Khan to setting her experiences down in gems. The birds-eye view of a rowing boat, with a team of rowers

N° 37

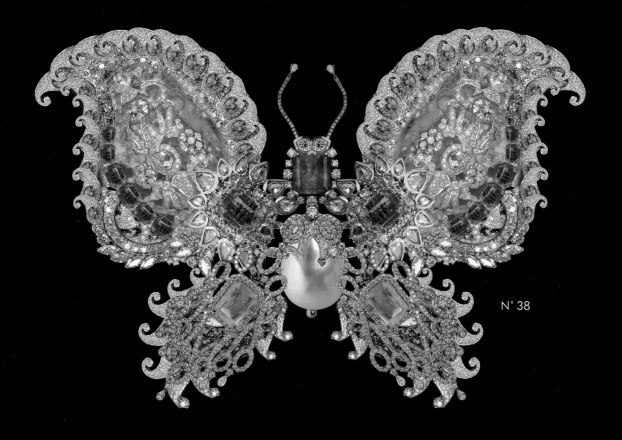

pulling on long oars, turns into a beautifully harmonised ruby and diamond bracelet, classical and symmetrical in style. Men dancing with swirls of fire are morphed into a pair of diamond hoop earrings, with flame red rubies set at the front. Khan learned

to execute and physically create Fine Jewellery by working with some of the top luxury jewellery houses in India, where she also learnt more about the traditional techniques of the craft. But it is still the artistic vision of what she sees every

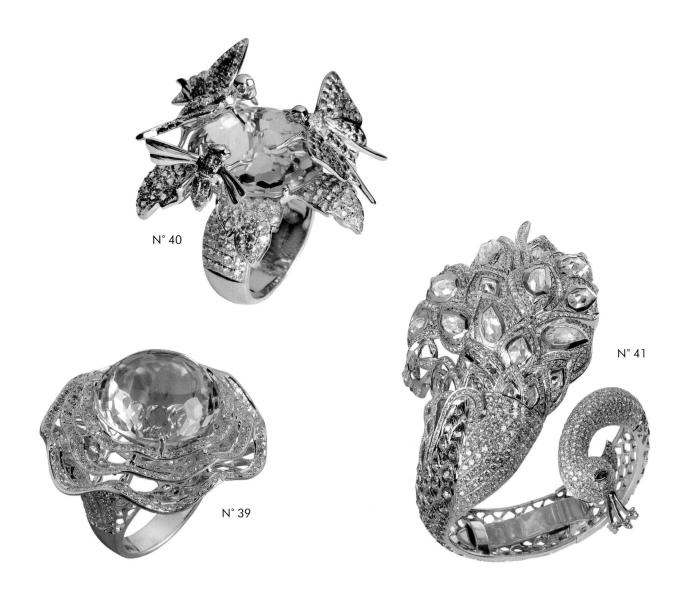

N° 40

N° 39

N° 41

day, combined with her own personal international style which lie at the heart of her exclusive jewels.

Personable and stylish, Farah started to gather personal clients as well. Her pieces are such showstoppers that it did not take long for this clientele to grow and she was eventually forced to open her own label. Born to a Bollywood family, the opening of her first boutique garnered a great deal of attention from locals. But it is her loyal collectors who give their full support for this independent designer. There is no typical Farah Khan collector. In fact, Khan has learned that women from all over the world have their own unique tastes and are always drawn to what they like. One European woman walked into the boutique in its early days, apparently dressed for an Ashram, wearing no jewels at all and who seemed to have just wondered in out of curiosity. She turned out to be one of Khan's key fans and left with half the pieces in the store.

Many of Khan's collectors come back for more, as they get so much attention from others when they wear the jewels. Similarly, they cater for women all over

N° 43

N° 44

N° 45

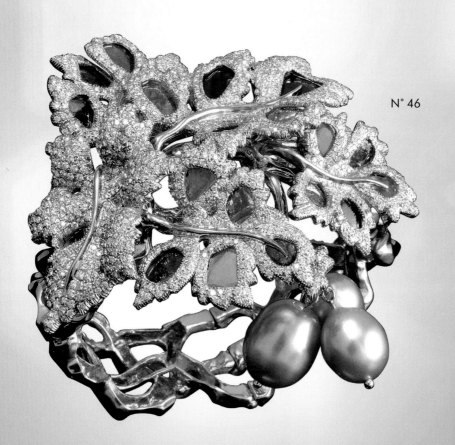

the world as they are crammed with layers of various cultural styles and influences. A recent masterpiece finished by Khan is a Chinese Dragon bracelet, to celebrate the year of the dragon. Taking eight months to create, the bangle is cast out of yellow gold, its body studded with diamond pave, and a patterned with layers of tanzanite beads and emerald cabochons down its back.

The size of the piece is significant and it is only due to Khan's experience in wax casting that she was able to create something so voluminous which is also light enough to wear comfortably. The

N° 47

dragon is meticulously detailed and opens easily due to a mechanism within the tail, allowing it to flip back and open for the wrist.

Khan misses the jewel acutely, as it sold within a week of completion. The designer had grown so attached to the dragon, she regrets letting it go so quickly. Nothing like it will be made again, as all of her masterpieces are unique.

The designer takes pride in all her jewels personally; they are like her children. She hopes that when they leave her they are loved and appreciated by the person wearing them. Khan makes *precious* become *priceless*.

JJBUCKAR

"WHEN WE EMBRACE CUTTING EDGE TECHNOLOGIES AND
MACHINERY WE TAKE QUALITY TO NEW HEIGHTS."

JACOB BUCKAREFF

Jacob Buckareff's atelier carved a large cocoon-shaped yellow amber. Upon completion he handed it to his wife, jewellery designer Julie Buckareff and asked her what she saw in the gem. Her immediate thoughts turned to a very large, fattened bug, not a creature found in nature but rather in a cartoon or caricature. Several sketches followed featuring such a character, busy in flight; its yellow gold wings sparkling with multi-coloured garnets and a blue sapphire *pavé* tie blowing with the speed of flight. Already the creature was animated. One finishing touch was added; a pair of flying goggles, in white gold and set with diamonds, and quartz crystal lenses. Drawn instantly to the loveable piece, a collector from Florida spotted it in their boutique and asked to hold it. Upon lifting it, he noticed that the *en tremblant* wings fluttered with the slightest movement, due to a delicate spring mechanism put in place by Jacob - the technical mastermind of the design

N° 48

N° 49

N° 50

duo. The collector felt affection for the jewel and instantly bought it for his cabinet at home. Seeing it every day in his home makes him smile. This is a typical story for JJBuckar. With Julie's uninhibited vision and Jacob's fascination with all things technical, they are able to create pieces which inspire their collectors on all levels. Jacob has a particular passion for intricate mechanisms, such as locks and hinges. Trained in his father's workshop as a watchmaker, he brings his obsession with mechanical challenges to work. Julie remembers a particular commission, for which she had designed a substantial pair of hooped earrings for a client who did not have pierced ears. Jacob puzzled over the conundrum for days before his *eureka*

N° 52

N° 51

N° 53

moment finally came, at which point he was able to race to their atelier and create his new invention: an ear-clip strong enough to support heavy earrings, without causing discomfort to the wearer. The same amount of thought goes into every one of their creations. One of their many award winning jewels, a cameo locket took more than 400 hours to create.

When Julie saw the beautiful cameo she instantly knew what she wanted to create; a sentimental jewel. A nest to symbolize a home and a locket to contain photographs of family and loved ones.

The locket was based around the design of a bird's nest down to the smallest details such as the placement of wires. The wires resemble how intricately the mother builds her nest, but demand far more technical precision and skill to create. Hundreds of red wires in varying thicknesses wrap around the cameo and maintain the

body of the piece. A hundred white gold leaves were then cut out and studded with diamonds, to cascade over the front and back of the piece. As with all the JJBuckar creations, the work is as intricate at the back as the front, and as perfect inside as out. Jacob's mechanical fingerprint is visible in the neatly hinged photo frames nestled tightly inside the locket and its engraved door which snaps shut decisively with the perfect 'click'.

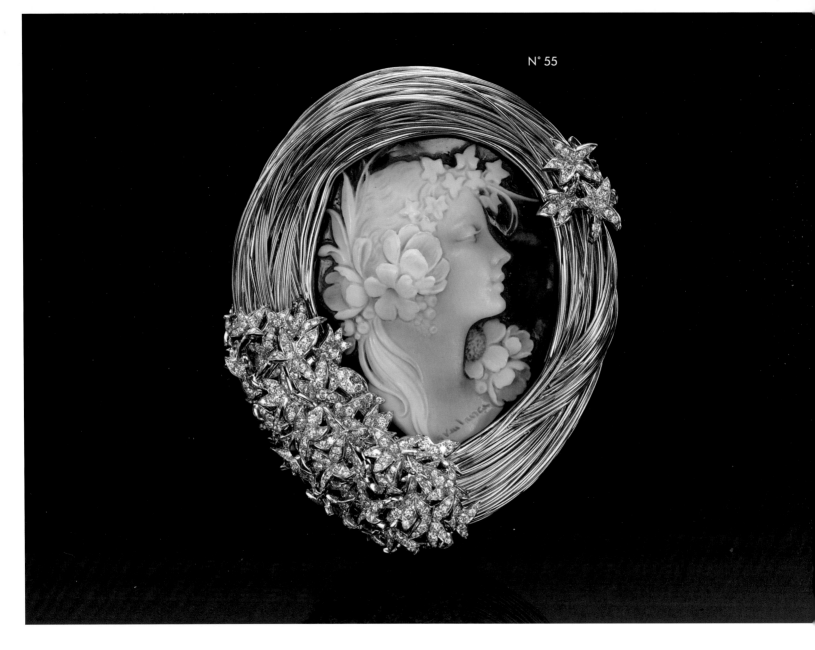

N° 56

LEVIEV

"BUYING JEWELLERY SHOULD BE A PLEASURE, AS IT IS NOT A NECESSITY."

RICHARD WEINBERG

A discrete boutique on London's Bond Street, Leviev's private showroom is one of only five retail destinations for the eminent jeweller. The showrooms and the stupendous jewels encased within them are only the tip of the iceberg for the substantial company. Leviev is one of the most diverse establishments in the gems and Fine Jewellery industry. Going back three generations, the Leviev brand has under its wing multiple operations in diamond mining, polishing and wholesaling, as well as their most recent venture: the creation of magnificent jewels. For collectors, the transition is an obvious one. Sourcing a 100ct or 50ct D-flawless diamond is a highly specialised process. Understanding how to set such a stone demands the same insight and expertise, with the creativity and technical *savoir-faire* to bring the gems to life in a single piece. Housed inside the intimate boutiques, Leviev offers an interpersonal and discreet carriage from the very first stage of the process to the last. It is not unusual for the showrooms to have walk-in clients ask to see a rare and

N° 57

generous stone, for which Leviev are prepared at all times, with vaults fully stocked with some of their choicest inventory. Few jewellery brands are this vertically integrated and able to provide jewels at every stage of development. Of these, Leviev is able to do it in by far the gentlest way.

Upon entering the Bond Street location, clients are immediately invited in as guests to look at the finished pieces already on display. Despite the value of the jewels,

N° 59

N° 60

N° 61

the staff is intentionally approachable, respecting how easy it is for customers to be intimidated by the grandeur of the inventory or the reputation of the brand. Friendly and helpful, they are eager to show off any jewels on display and explain the story behind them. In particular, a masterpiece which has attracted the attention of connoisseurs around the world is the *Yellow and White Diamond Scarf Necklace*: 267 diamonds of the highest quality drape-like silk in their barely visible platinum settings. Fine Jewellery of this quality needs handling to appreciate fully, and one does not need to pull up in a chauffeur driven Jaguar to be welcomed into the family fold.

New clients looking for a simple engagement ring at a modest price-point are given the same level of attention as a collector of 'investment worthy' gems.

Escorted upstairs and introduced to one of the proprietors, they are seated, offered a drink and entitled to as much uninterrupted time as they like with one of the company's trusted experts. Leviev may be a leader in the world of Fine Jewellery, but it is their service which makes them an invaluable addition to the tradition of Bond Street excellence.

MARGHERITA BURGENER

"MARGHERITA'S JEWELS ARE ADDICTIVE. THEY ARE NOT MY FIRST
CHOICE, BUT MY ONLY CHOICE."

TERRI C. THRASH

Leviathan gems are the stars of Margherita Burgener jewellery. Their designer, Emanuela Burgener is happy to let these shimmering stones take centre stage. A lovely Brazilian aquamarine drop, weighing an incredible 197.13 ct, is hung delicately from a barely seen white gold chain. The stone is supported almost invisibly by a diamond encrusted white gold band, tracing a swanlike glittering line around the sides of the faceted stone. Inviting light in from all angles, the gem comes alive, radiating reflected beams on the skin of its owner and creating a magical halo effect. Burgener rarely allows her gems to be encased in metal settings, as she travels extensively to find stones which are not only high in quality but also cut perfectly so that the gems appear to dance before your very eyes. Cocktail rings show the same reverence to the mystery of these coloured stones. Be it a Peridot, Tanzanite, Aquamarine or Amethyst, her centre stone is usually on show from all sides. Either through a delicate lattice of white gold circles or diamond *pavé* set gold leaves, the depth of a Burgener gem is mesmerising through the shank of her bold, contemporary cocktail rings.

Despite her obsession with travelling to source the right stones, it is the craftsmanship of her workshop team which makes it possible to both expose the stones and then place them in such original designs. Burgener is able to experiment with her techniques as she oversees every stage of production in her workshop in Valenza which has been part of her family for generations.

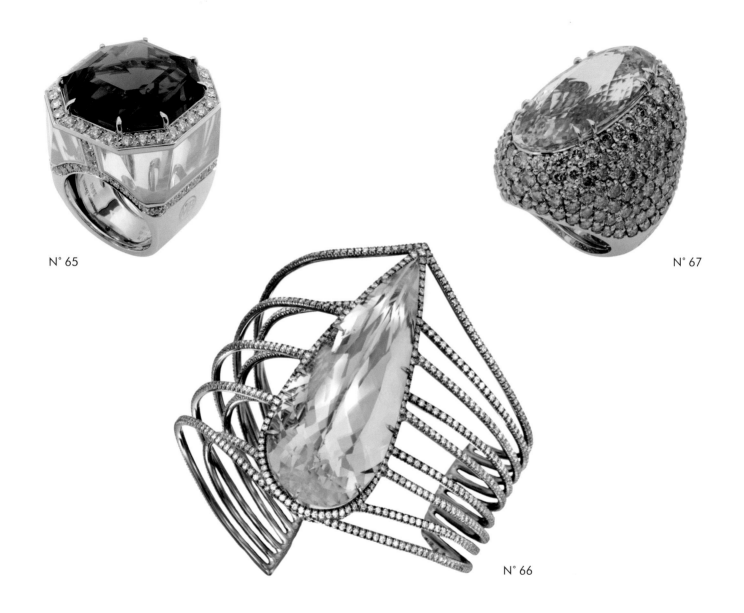

N° 65

N° 67

N° 66

From the melting of the precious metals to setting the stones, it is a process the artist has been watching and learning for 30 years now.

Now named after her eldest daughter, the Margherita Burgener label is known for its one-of-a-kind or limited edition contemporary pieces. Her fearless vision and passion for feminine, coloured gems often lead her to more unusual materials, such as titanium which is used to set an 85.17 ct Pink Morganite in the centre of a cuff. The natural grey metal formed the design of the cuff, which consisted of multiple thread-thin bands studded with diamonds, wrapping around the wrist. Titanium was also used to show off the designer's technical mastery in her *Felci earrings* - an accurate illustration of two feathers sketched in diamonds, gold and titanium.

These technically demanding pieces are often snapped up by the top auction houses, such as Sotheby's, Phillips de Pury and Christie's, whose international clients are looking to add something beautiful but original to their collections of jewels. Others prefer to approach the designer herself for a bespoke piece. Either way, a Margherita Burgener jewel is a lifetime investment and a stunning party piece.

MICHAEL YOUSSOUFIAN

"I'M ALWAYS LOOKING AHEAD TO GO FURTHER, TO BETTER
MYSELF IN MY PASSION, EXCELLENCE IS KEY."
MICHAEL YOUSSOUFIAN

Out of the blue Michael Youssoufian received a letter from a man he had never met. The man was an eminent American collector of Fine Art and jewellery and had happened to see some of the designer's work by chance. The gentleman wished to know if it was possible to send over a sample of his own gem collection, so that the jeweller might be able to create something interesting out of them. Intrigued, the designer agreed to see the stones. A box arrived containing 30kg of gems, with the further instructions that the designer was to do exactly as he wished with them. Every gem was of top quality; the variety was endless. Youssoufian worked on the commission for three years. It was only upon delivering the first batch of couture jewels that he met his humble patron. It is a story worthy of an *Arabian Nights Tale* but the Youssoufian family have a rich history in the fine jewellery industry and many similar stories to match it. Michael's grandfather was the personal jeweller to the Royal Court of Egypt, His

N° 69

N° 70

Royal Highness King Fouad and later, King Farouk. Naturally, the jewels created for such collectors were serious pieces; both traditional and also in the latest styles. Large, important gems needed setting and the Youssoufian family was charged with this task.

After the abdication, however the Youssoufian family left Egypt. Geneva was the obvious place to open a shop, due to the sophisticated tastes of the locals and the strength of the jewellery and fine watches sector.

N° 71   N° 72   N° 73

N° 74

N° 75

Michael has worked in every part of the fine jewellery industry. He trained in the French tradition of fine jewellery making, worked in Geneva crafting timepieces for luxury brands and has also spent several years in gem polishing and manufacturing, cutting gems to bring out their best colour and clarity.

However, it is his training in Fine Art -specifically painting - which inspires his work more than all the skills of a jeweller. His collected expertise, in gems and precious metals only serves as a way to make his visions become a reality. He loves to paint with gems, as though on a canvas, and it is this unusual lack of favouritism towards the more precious stones over other equally beautiful gems, which make his work so special to behold. For Youssoufian the first stage of creating any piece is simply to collect enough of

the right gems to start designing a multi-gem piece. It could be an array of colours and tones, such as deep purples, pinks and blues or vast collections of green stones, which come together to create the correct palette for the designer to start working. It can take a decade or more to reach this early stage but the designer is aided in his patience by his great love of gemstones. The conch pearls used in his flower brooches were with him

N° 77

for over 10 years, as the inspiration for a design had not reached him. All the designs Youssoufian creates need to be, by his own standard, worthy of the gems he has collected for so long. It is when he believes that a piece can do justice to his collection, and only then, that he will begin production. He will then set the stones in the manner of a collage, much like an impressionist painter used specks of paint to create an overall effect, regularly taking the pieces apart many times until the composition is perfect.

A Youssoufian piece is mouth-watering when completed. A green cabochon bracelet sparkles like a magical landscape; a pair of faceted ruby earrings cascade down like a fountain of colour; a small ring is clustered with conch pearls at the centre

N° 79

and then opens out into fluorescent petals and leaves.

All his gems seem alive thanks to his meticulous settings, which allow as much light to shine through the gem from behind as possible. It creates a kaleidoscopic effect which is mesmerising. The movement of the gems is equally important. The designer is so inspired by the women who wear his jewels; he always allows them to dance happily on the wearer if they are chandelier earrings. In the case of a necklace or a bracelet, he prefers the piece to drape over the neck or wrist of his clients, so that they don't encumber but sit like a piece of clothing.

A piece of clothing embedded with jewels, worthy of an *Arabian Nights Tale*.

THE
ROMANTICS

CINDY CHAO

"CINDY CHAO EPITOMISES THE ART JEWEL."
ANONYMOUS COLLECTOR

Countless artists and poets over time have looked to the sublime beauty of nature for inspiration. Few are able to surpass it. Cindy Chao's jewels have the ability to capture all of her organic subjects in a brief moment in time and enhance their every detail, making them sparkle in the process. Her work is nature under a microscope, and it makes for exquisite jewels. The secret to Chao's definitive style is her heritage. The daughter of a sculptor, Chao spent her early years sitting in her father's studio, working with clay and wax. This same technique is used in her precious jewellery. The wax model follows the original sketch. With the wax between her nimble fingers, Chao is able to twist and manipulate forms with all the confidence of a sculptor. All her jewels work as three-dimensional objects in their own right. They dance and move in all directions, without being confined by symmetry or straight lines. When the wax is finally replaced by a sparkling white or yellow gold

N° 80

and is set, creating the finished jewel, the metal still appears to flow in liquid form. For Chao, stone setting is just as laboured. Even the *pavé* work is not simply a glittering surface embedded with standardised stones. They are of various sizes, shapes and tones, giving the jewels a texture and variation rarely seen in fine jewellery. Larger white diamonds are also used to interrupt *pavé* set surfaces, resembling a dew drop or a layer of frost on a flower- no wonder these magnificent objects take two years to create.

As a trained gemologist, Chao also has an

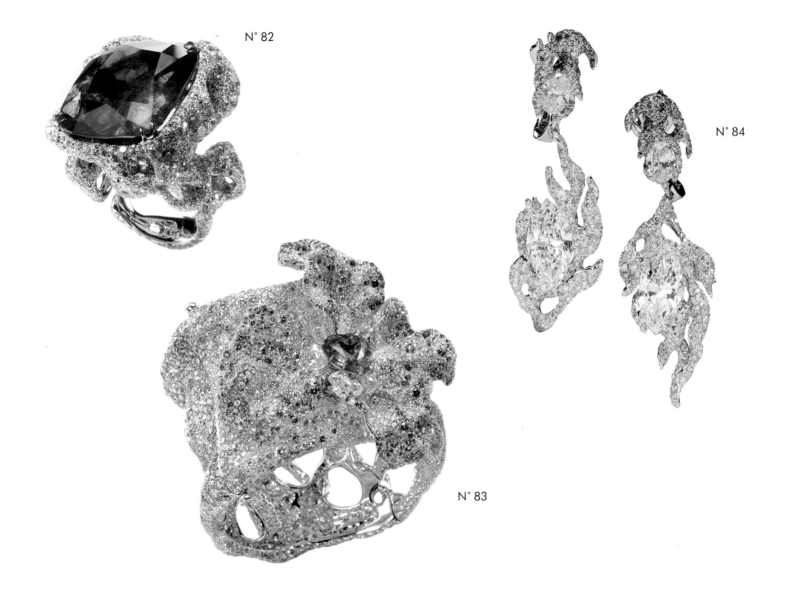

N° 82

N° 83

N° 84

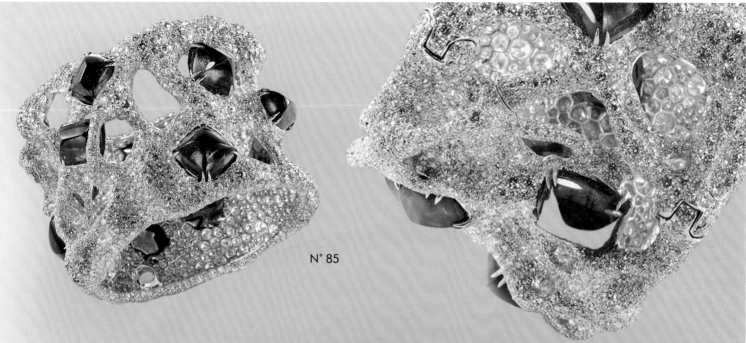

unapologetic love for giant centre stones. Her emerald and diamond drop earrings carry a pair of stunning 63 carat emeralds; a feat to obtain for a small independent designer. They would perfectly match her *Emerald City* ring which has a 44 carat emerald at its heart.

Securing a private appointment with the designer is notably difficult due to her only creating 36 masterpieces a year. She is a magnet for serious collectors thanks to her combination of artistic temperament and her use of substantial gems.
Pieces move quickly however and this is

why when an auction house like Christie's or Sotheby's manages to woo the designer into offering one of her masterpieces to their fine jewellery auctions, people line up to view the piece and bidders create quite a stir in the auction room. Now the designer has been forced to create a *White Label* collection which is available internationally in various luxury stores.

Museums are also desperate to secure her work for their private collections. Most notably, The Smithsonian Institute's National Museum of Natural History has given Chao's *Royal Butterfly* pride of place

in its collection of gems. Chao creates one of her celebrated butterflies once a year. This masterpiece features 2,318 gems including a pair of rough diamonds on the scales and, of course, intricate details on the back. The jewel puts the museum's *Butterfly Garden* soulfully in the shade.

FABIO SALINI

"THE VALUE OF A PIECE IS THE RICHNESS OF ITS ELEMENTS; THE BALANCE OF THE GOLDSMITH'S ART, CREATIVITY AND DESIGN."

FABIO SALINI

During his stretch at Cartier and Bulgari, Fabio Salini learned a great deal about luxury fine jewellery design. In particular, he learned about quality in production being the most important measure of a jewel. The other was how to create volume in a design. Sculpting work like the famous Cartier (tiger) panther or a Bulgari serpent means taking a multi-dimensional approach to design. Even if a jewel is only visible from the front, it is generous from the sides. These are the lessons the Rome-based designer took with him when starting out at the turn of the Millennium, to create his own line. There the similarities end. Fabio Salini is one of the most experimental living jewellers in the world. Much like Fulco Verdura in the mid 20th century, Fabio Salini is not intimidated by the preciousness of his gems, and loves to combine them with non-precious materials to see how they look and behave. The result is a fascinating array of

N° 86

N° 88

N° 87

artistic pieces with every combination one can imagine. Anything which can be done with precious gems and look beautiful, he seems to have done: diamonds have been sewn (set) onto silk (tassels) for long drop earrings; gems have been attached to crocodile leather; cuffs wrapped in high-grade *Galuchat* and complimented with solid gold and gems, necklaces made from ivory, these are just some of the daring creations Fabio Salini has added to his repertoire of jewels in the past decade.

N° 89

N° 91

N° 90

Despite the rare blend of materials all the pieces have a distinct classical quality. Perhaps it is the production values or the requisite volume within the designs. All the pieces sit as comfortably with collectors as their more traditional jewellery.

Primarily it is about balance and proportion. Fabio Salini does not use a material because he wants something new to play with. Rather, he approaches the design from the opposite angle. He decides the effect he wants and then discovers the suitable materials to work with. In this way, no matter what his jewels are sculpted from, their composition is always perfect and the result is always surprisingly pretty. Beholders of Fabio Salini's jewellery, within seconds of seeing his work for the first time, are converted to his aesthetic, wondering why such things have not been done before.

The answer lies in Fabio Salini's traditional background and training. He learned the rules stringently before he began to break them. His consistent experimentation is always about seeing how far he can go technically, whilst still creating exquisite pieces. The gemologist-designer's popular rock crystal jewels are a perfect example of the classicism of the cutting edge designer; he carves out nuggets of rock crystal and embeds coloured gems inside them, to transmit transparency and luminosity. The lightness of these jewels and their fashionable colour combinations make them the prettiest and most fashionable collection of contemporary jewellery, since Verdura's stint at Chanel.

MING

"YOU CAN'T HELP BUT FEEL SPECIAL WHEN YOU WEAR
SOMETHING SHE HAS MADE."

MING COLLECTOR

London-based Ming Lampson is a renowned designer of fine jewellery. She specialises in ready-to-wear collections and sumptuous one-off pieces that are coveted by collectors across the world. Over the last eighteen years Ming has been making jewellery for an ever increasing loyal following and is, according to *Harper's Bazaar*, "an exceptional jewellery talent". Ming's themed collection 'Asian Princess' is inspired by the opulent symbolism of eastern cultures. Large emeralds drop from elegant Maharajan earrings, hand-carved gold and coral flowers dance across the hand and dragons, *pavé* set with hundreds of diamonds, chase rubies and Tahitian pearls. Ming has an obsession with rare and beautiful gemstones and their interplay with precious metal – the sparkle of yellow diamonds against rich yellow gold or the drama of vivid blue sapphires in blackened gold. Her one-off pieces often feature unusual coloured stones - champagne and peach sapphires, crysoberyl cat's eye, raw emerald crystals,

N° 96

a slither of imperial jade. Her one-off pieces range from extraordinary diamond necklaces to ornate octopus earrings and distinctive, elegant engagement rings. Each piece tells a story unique to the client. The octopus earrings were commissioned by a lady whose late father was a marine biologist.

The work proved nearly impossible for the designer, from a technical point of view. The creatures, when Ming drew them, looked wonderful but she needed to craft them in metal enamel and diamonds in a way that made sure the octopuses remained animated, but not too heavy to wear.

N° 97

N° 98

N° 99

N° 100

These superb earrings are now a favourite piece of Ming's. The technical frustrations were overcome and she managed to create a pair of asymmetrical octopuses that both draw constant attention from onlookers and reflect a very private feeling for the wearer.

Ming has a strong Notting Hill following, so it is no surprise that she set up her synonymous atelier here in 2005. The famous London borough has always been her base, but she wanted to combine her workshop with an Art Deco wood panelled shop that reflects early 5th Avenue style and 1920's Parisian glamour. The wood and the mirrors create a very private but inspirational space in which to discuss bespoke commissions with clients. Ming is uniquely qualified as a designer, skilled jeweller, gemologist and diamond appraiser, combining her artistic instinct with vigorous training and the use of challenging techniques.

All her jewellery is handmade in platinum and 18ct gold with craftsmanship of the finest quality, reflecting her firm belief that every piece passing through her hands may be regarded as 'future treasure.'

NICHOLAS VARNEY

"IT IS SO IMPORTANT FOR ME TO TRAVEL. AS THE LIGHT
CHANGES, SO DO THE IDEAS AND PALETTES IN MY MIND."

NICHOLAS VARNEY

Nicholas Varney's clients will already own diamonds. They will already have pearls and precious stones set demurely in platinum and gold, passed down from family members, or kept in a vault for formal occasions, when protocol forbids anything loud. When they visit Varney, it is for jewellery they can enjoy. Seeking new expression though colour they sort through his collection of weird and wonderful gemstones, searching for new ideas and the stories behind them. Varney is an explorer of stones with an ardent passion for adventure travel and unspoilt nature. This is highlighted in his work and for Varney, gems are more precious for having come out of the earth. He is not insistent on polishing and shaping stones into standard shapes and sizes. In fact, the New York based designer is known for creating jewels that work around the natural shapes and formations that appear in gems. His blue *Brick* bracelet is the perfect example of how the artist can collect gems, much like a child collects shells from the seashore, and turn them into

N° 102

magnificently refined pieces of jewellery. Thirty-five unique brick shapes are comprised of natural black Penn shell pearls and free form fire opals, all unique in shape, size and natural inflections. Varney encases each 'brick' in yellow or white gold and oxidised silver, *pavé* set in diamonds, tsavorite garnets and sapphires and finished off with his signature yellow gold grill setting at the back of each piece, swirling in a bow motif. These individual bricks form a flexible cuff bracelet that never ceases to amaze spectators. Each

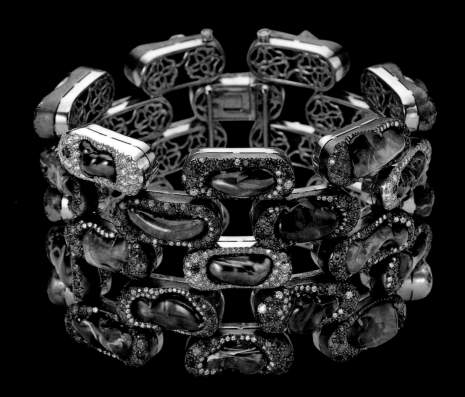

N° 103

N° 104

N° 105

N° 106

segment is different; each gem has been treated according to its requirements. This is the work of a designer who cares little for supercilious labels such as 'precious' or 'semi-precious'. If a gem is beautiful, if it works within the object, nothing else matters.

The result is a collection of one-off pieces ablaze with colour, harnessing stones many collectors have never heard of: Fire opals in deep blue and orange, pink conch pearls and Burmese spinel cabochons in pinks and purples, blue moonstones, purple quahog pearls and lemon chrysoprase.

Varney does use diamonds as accents and admits to a weakness for sapphires, although he prefers the stone in a lighter blue, rather than the deep tones coveted by investors. It has to be said that the way Varney feels about gems and jewels is infectious. All his collectors are repeat customers and become more open to the adventure of working with him as time goes on. The jewels are not for shrinking violets, however. One piece was returned to Varney a few days after purchase: A stingray brooch formed around a unique South Sea Pearl. It turns out the brooch was too overpowering for the women's purposes. In fact, no greater compliment could be given to an artist like Nicholas Varney. Thrilled to have the brooch back, he now keeps it in his own collection and has every intention of holding onto it.

POONAM SONI

"SONI BRINGS AN ARTIST'S EYE FOR COLOUR, DETAIL AND IMAGINATION TO HER MAGNIFICENT ONE-OF-A-KIND PIECES."

MICHAEL KORS

Early in her career, Poonam Soni created a gold bracelet carved with Greek and Egyptian handcrafted motifs with a malachite base & black onyx accents. The bracelet was bought by Sigi Walters, a winner of the *Miss Germany* title. Falling passionately in love with it, she sent a personal friend to India just to pick up the jewel. Such is the power of a Soni piece. The Designer enjoys creating traditional wedding jewellery. Her *trousseau* pieces are innovative and fusion, breaking away from the traditional style. Even the use of exotic *vilandi* or *minakari* is in a contemporary style infusing motifs of crushed gold - studded animals on strong colours of carved jade and deep blue Kyanite. A bride who has 80 pieces of the designer swears that you can recognise a Soni piece from a mile. Hailing from a country rich in fine jewellery tradition, Soni always desired to create something unique. In 1989, Soni brought in ground-breaking designs and introduced concepts of custom designing and bespoke jewellery to a closed Indian market. Generally families would order 5 pieces of the same

N° 108

design if they had five daughters in the family but Soni wanted to create statement pieces which would be unique to each woman. This prompted her to experiment with unusual styles and techniques. She set a trend for high-end fusion jewellery which has become her staple. Her statement one-of-a-kind pieces are worn by glamorous women worldwide and she designs exclusively for the discerning customer in Monte Carlo, Paris, and the royal families of the East. High-end fusion jewellery has become her staple.

N° 109

N° 110

N° 111

N° 112

Despite her contemporary edge, the Indian influences in Soni's jewellery are everywhere. She loves the Mogul style of fusing gold on glass and the traditional Bikaner *Vilandi* which she has used on the flat cut diamonds and traditional *Minakari* in her range of cuffs, which incorporate hand painted canvas in bright motifs depicting horses & cheetahs. Her new collection called *Gaudí Revived* uses a mixture of precious metals and plexiglass to recreate a groundbreaking mosaic effect. 'Itai Doshin', a *Falcon Lariat* was recently auctioned by Mark Poltimore at Sotheby's by Eco Art and Prince Albert II of Monaco. It is a dual purpose ornament inspired by the Saker Falcon that can be used as either a brooch or a lariat.

Other curious concoctions from the artist include a bespoke necklace designed out of gold coins. The task was to create something stylish yet understated with this many gold coins. Linking the coins together with hand painted Indian deities on glass in bronze colours, she enamelled and textured the coins in rust brown enamel to tone them down. The entire effect was sensational and the same client has now given the designer another sack of gold coins, for the designer to create something for her daughter.

N° 114

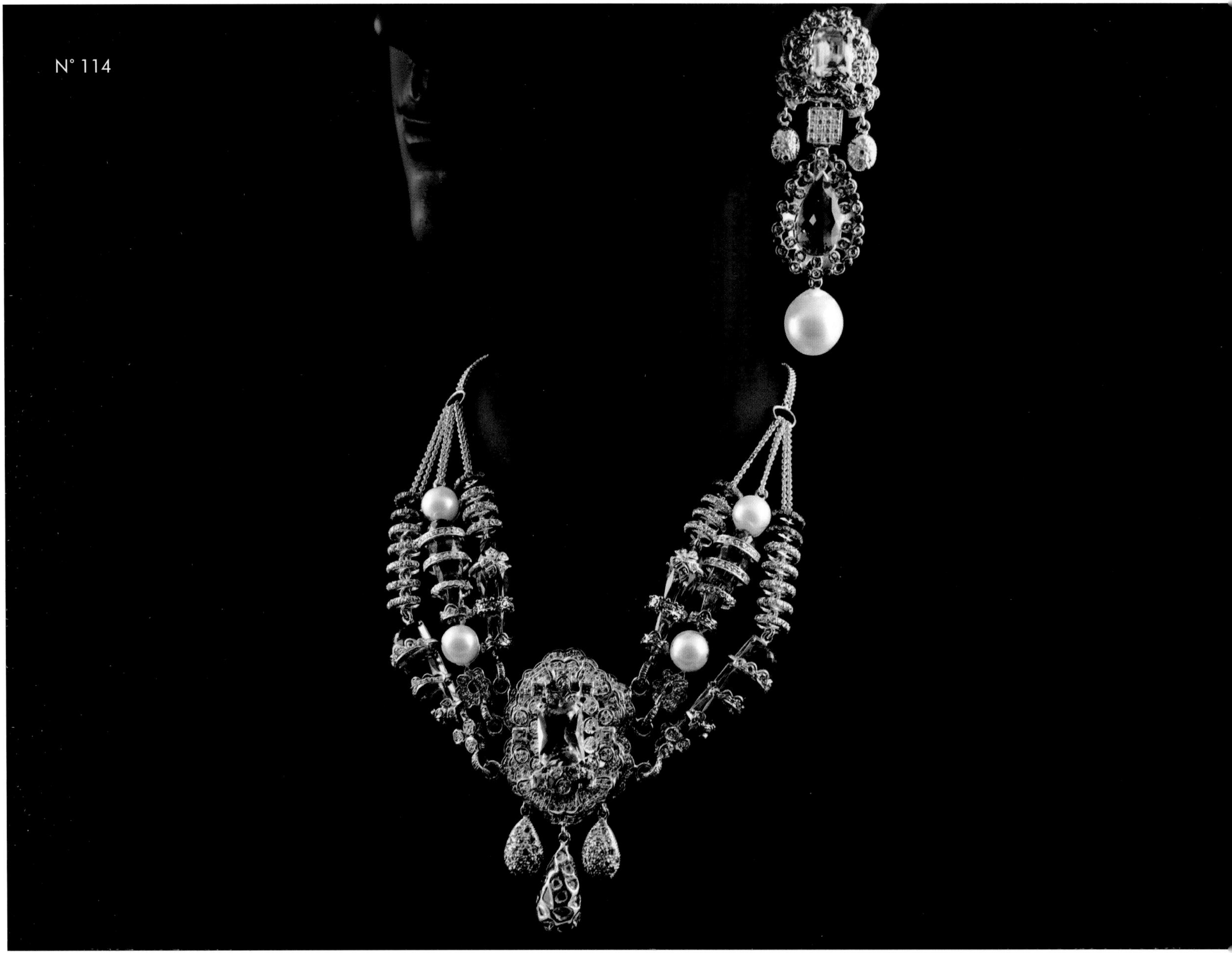

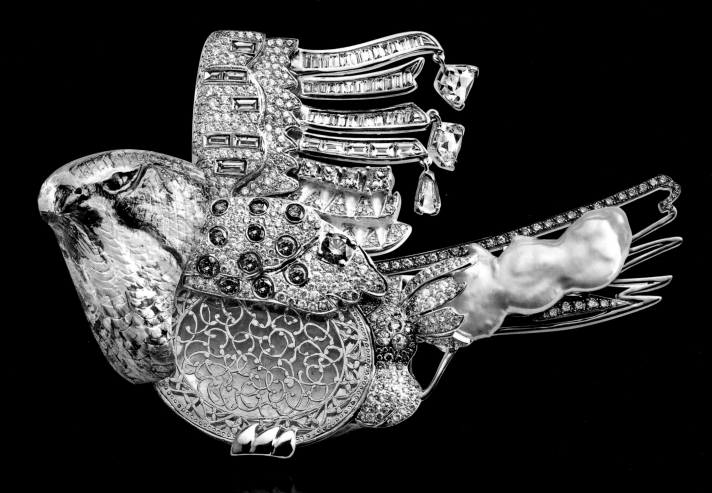

THE
STORYTELLERS

THE STORYTELLERS

YEWN

"THE BEST CONTEMPORARY CHINESE DESIGN I HAVE SEEN SINCE
THE END OF CHINESE MONARCHY!"

MICHELLE OBAMA

Dickson Yewn is a rare gem: a contemporary designer and conceptual artist who is not afraid to pay allegiance to the past. As masterpieces of Contemporary Chinese design, his jewels are often embedded with secret messages, Eastern philosophy, symbols and icons which are not conspicuous but are etched within the framework of the piece or are integrated into the complex lattice structure of a ring. In addition to these references, Yewn often draws on ancient Chinese arts, such as the intricate enamelling *Cloisonné* technique used on ceremonial vases from the culturally rich Ching Dynasty. Instead of using enamel, Yewn creates the same effect using gemstones, embedded within each gold *cloison*. The effect is a meticulously delicate collection of jewels, which include a yellow gold cuff with the *cloisons* outlining peonies around the bracelet. The signature works of the designer however are his collectable lattice rings. Distinctly modern in appearance, these cubic lattice pieces are, in fact inspired by traditional Chinese architecture.

N° 116

The *Wish Fulfilling Lattice* ring, in particular, uses the carved wooden windows found in these buildings as the design for the trellis which makes up the structure of the ring's square facades. Upon closer inspection, the ring also depicts the Mandarin phrase for "As You Wish", to bring fortune to the person wearing the jewel.

To own one of Dickson's jewels would be fortunate, indeed.

N° 117

LORENZ BÄUMER

"JEWELLERY SO DISTINCTIVE TO THE INDIVIDUAL; EVEN IF THEY'RE NOT WEARING IT, ONE COULD KNOW WHOM IT BELONGS TO."

LORENZ BÄUMER

Coveted by industry insiders for decades, the name Lorenz Bäumer has remained a secret to collectors until relatively recently. Bäumer's designs have not. Creating original and ground breaking designs for Baccarat and Chanel Fine Jewellery for years, this artist trained as an engineer and studied architecture before setting foot in the gems and jewellery world. The influence on his work is visible. Despite his often witty, colourful designs featuring his less than romantic subjects, such as artichokes, leeks and tomatoes, the artist has a unique confidence in the simplicity of line. A single gold slim band weaves round the finger tracing a heartbeat reading on a heart monitor, a clever twist on the language of love. Slightly more elaborate, the designer's *Noeud* (knot) and *Barbelé* (barbed wire) rings are also popular amongst Parisian collectors for their clean statements - perfect for every day. Unpretentious to the last, yet fiercely coveted, Bäumer has mastered the art of creating sumptuous jewels which can be worn with a wink and a smile. His recent masterpiece, an aigrette for

N° 118

the new Grimaldi bride, Charlene of Monaco on the evening of her wedding, Bäumer proves that he is the man to go to for an informal reinterpretation of high jewellery. An apologetic variation on the tiara, the tiara was inspired by the Australian princess' love of the ocean. A spray of white gold and diamonds, it can be worn as a hair clip, a brooch or full headpiece.

N° 119

THEO FENNELL

"WE REALLY ARE AT THE VANGUARD OF THE RENAISSANCE OF ONE-OFF, HAND-MADE JEWELLERY."

THEO FENNELL

Above his flagship store in London's Fulham Road, Theo Fennell and his dedicated team of master craftsmen weave magical tales of adventure, mystery and romance into intricate miniatures to adorn his faithful clients. The story begins with one of many casual sketches: black ink on the pages of Fennell's omnipresent notepads. These renderings vary from faces, flowers and landscapes to designs for silverware and jewellery. Each study draws on real life and the designer's encyclopaedic knowledge of visual motifs, symbolism and icons curated from craftsmen throughout history. The *Fleur De Lys* and *Napoleonic Bee* have taken inspiration from France; dragons and secret Oriental Gardens are influences from the Far East whilst oversized drop earrings have been borrowed from Elizabethan portraits. An array of bedevilled hearts and an extensive range of crosses and keys, all in a variety of shapes, styles, precious materials and sizes add to the collections. Even the faces of saints and sinners, such as

N° 120

Ghandi and Chairman Mao in the *Heroes and Villains* series are duly moulded into rings for Theo Fennell's collectors. As well as abstractions and the extraordinary inventions of his imagination there appears to be no symbol, amulet, icon or design in the annals of history which this British jeweller has not incorporated into his work. One of Fennell's most enduring motifs is the skull. Due to the innate gothic rock & roll influences tied to skulls and black rhodium plated metals, Theo Fennell has helped to forge the way forward for fine jewellery in a younger generation. For his team of

N° 121

N° 122

N° 123

N° 124

YELLOW &
BLACK RHODIUM
IN
BLOSSOM

DIA

DOOR
TO
OPEN

PINK
GOLD
DOOR

BAMBOO
EDGE

SEE
ENAMEL
PICTURE

N° 125

craftsmen, it is also an opportunity to show off their skills in moulding perfect multi-dimensional designs; with *pavé* set snakes weaving through hollow eye sockets. For the designer, this continual reference to death is happily intertwined with his fascination with life and the many layers of history and culture fossilised in his work.

Much like the *Vanitas* paintings of Holbein and his contemporaries, Fennell's pieces create narratives by gathering a multiple of seemingly unrelated symbols from cultures past and present. Combined, they portray the key theme throughout

his work: that everyone and everything is equalised by death.

The latest collection of masterpieces is the most explicit treatment of this theme. *Sic Transit Gloria Mundi* (How Fleeting Are Earth's Glories) is a series of iconic brooches featuring busts of characters such as Shakha Zulu, Elizabeth I, Cleopatra and Chief Sitting Bull. Due to the complexity of these pieces, it takes the varied skills of some eight craftsmen to create the one-off brooches. The hand engraved gold casings, enamelling and carved gemstones beautifully represent the grandeur of these

characters in all their finery. The beautifully detailed backs are works of art in their own right. In true Theo Fennell fashion, the busts are completed with the exposed skulls of those long gone, carved from mammoth bone, black spinel and moonstones, a witty but wise reminder that even the great and the good must ultimately meet their end.

N° 126

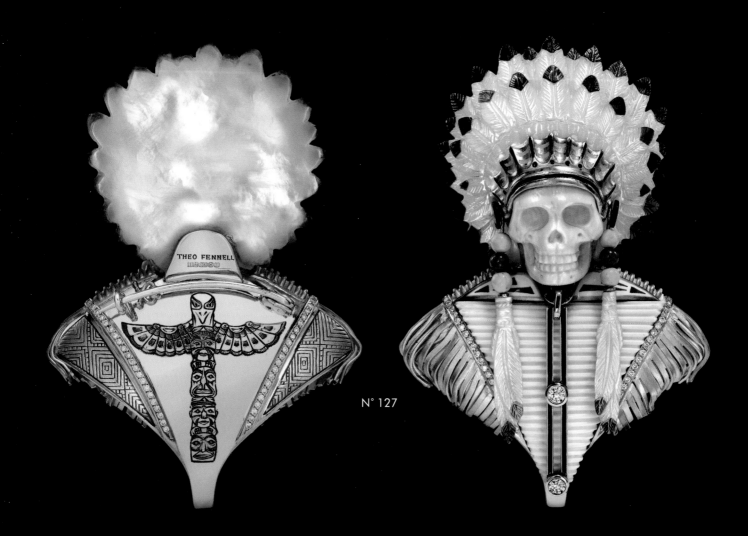

N° 127

VICENTE GRACIA

"HIS PIECES TELL STORIES, HIDE SECRETS; THEY GIVE SHAPE TO
FANTASY AND TO THE ROOTS OF A CULTURE."

ANONYMOUS COLLECTOR

It was love at first sight, when Vicente Gracia first set foot inside Granada's Alhambra Palace. For the young, romantic son of a traditional Spanish goldsmith and jeweller, this fairytale palace with its gem-encrusted walls and historical ceilings, was the perfect inspiration for a collection of fine jewellery. The Valencian artist-jeweller sculpts his work in much the same way as a mason or an architect. He sketches passionately, usually inspired by a narrative, such as the Persian poems of Omar Khayyam and Hafez and Rumi or historical tales of chivalry and knights in shining armour. Woven into his work is the same blend of Moorish, European and Mediterranean stylistic reference that emanates from the streets of Valencia. Gracia delights in the conflict of all these styles which ultimately converge in the architecture of the town, to create such a beautifully mystical place. Vicente's jewels hold the same power over his collectors. His clients often take the opportunity to travel to the Mediterranean

N° 128

town as Vicente's guests in his boutique hotel, to commission a piece from the artist himself - all part of the experience. The workshop is packed with historic regalia - from suits of armour through to volumes of illustrated books from all ages.

His clients are lured into his fairytale world, watching the artist at work on his poetic pieces and begging him to tell their own stories through his jewels. An avid Gracia collector from California commissioned the tale of *The Nightingale and The Rose* in the form of a ring. As a child, she was read this ancient oriental story by her

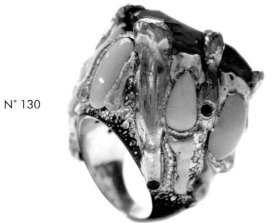

N° 130

N° 132

N° 131

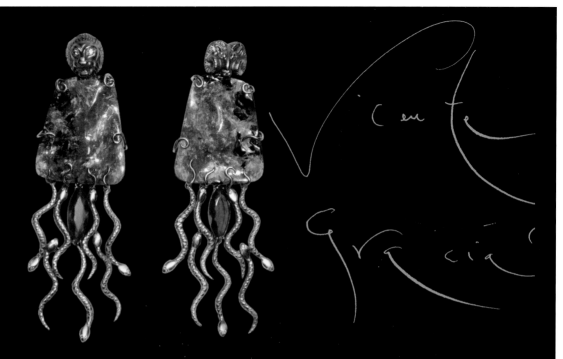

father at bedtime. The jeweller was of course thrilled to take on the fantastical commission.

Thanks to the warmth and tactile nature of his work, its earthiness and touching naïvety, a Vicente Gracia piece could easily be mistaken for a recently discovered ancient artefact. This is no accident. Despite learning his craft from his father - a creator of more classic pieces - his artistic direction is deliberately raw, employing techniques used in Valencia since the Roman period and favouring 24k unpolished gold for his creations.

His artisans have been working at their craft for 40 years and are part of the Gracia family. They're every bit as passionate about experimenting with techniques as Gracia. In particular, his enamelling, which is a signature of his work, adds explosions of colour like the glossy tiles in Spanish architecture.

Often, the gold appears to have been sculpted much like putty or clay, the mark of the artist's tools still visible on the matt surface. Even the celebrated Gracia logo is roughly stamped on the jewels, as though done with an ancient branding tool. Gracia describes his collectors as "women who do not like jewellery in the conventional sense, but are seeking artistic objects rather than ostentatious ones". Primarily, they purchase his pieces because they love them. After all, the Spanish for jewellery is *joya*, which also means joy.

WENDY YUE

"HER INTENSE IMAGINATION, EXQUISITE CRAFTSMANSHIP AND HUMOUR MAKE EACH CREATION A TRUE MASTERPIECE."

ANNOUSHKA DUCAS, OWNER ANNOUSHKA, LONDON

Fairytales are not for children, as Wendy Yue's international cult following demonstrates. Her following of supremely fashionable and forward-thinking ladies adore her for the avant-garde vision she brings to fine jewellery. The designer's signature blackened gold and deep moody hues lend her fantastical backdrops a dusky romance that is rarely represented in high jewellery. Yue rarely falls back on sugary pastel tones. She eschews the sweetness of fairies and butterflies for bats, frogs, monkeys and other animated creatures. Even her depiction of traditional subjects such as flowers are not left to sit quietly as static ornaments; rather, their brambles are made wild, twisting freely round the jewels, forming rings and cuffs. Beautiful gem carved buds are crushed under the weight of lizards and snakes, or else they bloom in gigantic bejewelled renderings on a cuff, creating a breathtakingly dramatic effect. Yue's pieces are instantly recognisable for their larger-than-life presence. Inspired by her own travels, the Hong Kong based designer created jewels

N° 134

for other brands before deciding to set up her own *atelier* and production workshop. Free from the rules and regulations of traditional design houses, Yue's unique take on nature and her achievements reverberated throughout the collectors' world.

The artist loves to play with dimensions, crafting huge cocktail rings and statement cuffs elaborately laboured with layers of contrasting gems and techniques. The look is modern, edgy, even daring, yet imbued with tradition. Yue's pieces are created much like miniature sculptures, incorporating gem carvings, cameos, unusual pearls, enamelling and even elaborately carved jade into the richly

N° 135

N° 136

N° 137

N° 138

layered pieces. It is the juxtaposition between the traditional oriental craftsmanship and the bold contemporary aura of the pieces which make them so irresistible to European and American collectors. The Eastern imagery is not lost on the women, either. Frogs are a chosen favourite of the designer as it is supposed to bring luck to the wearer. The Eastern temple masterpieces have proved some of her most popular works to date, and her animated Buddha's feature regularly in the collections.

This adds a distinctly exotic flavour to everything Yue brings to life, but it's the elaborate narrative tradition of Eastern sculpture which stands out in all her work. All the jewels are sparkling elaborate tales.

Her natural landscapes are taken from wild forests and exotic jungles. Her flowers and fauna continue to dance round each piece, even once out of sight, at the side of a ring, or the back of a bracelet, much as they would do in real life.

Even architecturally inspired pieces are given a magical lease of life in the form of a dragon perching on the roof of a temple or a pagoda hosting a garden party for seven children, each representing one of the gods of the elements. The details are infinite in this collection of jewels, making them pleasing to the eye. Much like a classical fairytale, they continue to thrill and inspire every time they are revisited and, like traditional fables, they will last for generations.

THE
ALCHEMISTS

The Alchemists

SHAWISH

"TO CREATE THE PERFECT DIAMOND RING IS THE EPITOME OF ART."

Mohamed Shawesh

The unsung heroes of the Fine Jewellery world are the lapidaries. Everyone loves a glittering gem in a jewel, be it a dramatic necklace, a statement cuff or a cocktail ring. However, the sculpted metal framework in which the jewel sits and the arrangement of the collection of gems garners more attention to the design of the stone itself. Most collectors of jewellery will be used to seeing a jewel finished and polished, beautifully presented in its velveteen box. Yet gems in their raw state look vaguely similar to a rock. It is the job of the lapidary to take the stone, and cut it with such mathematical precision that the muddy, earthy stone turns into a brilliant light-infused and colourful gem. It flatters the person wearing it and makes them look like a million dollars – or rather like 70 million dollars in the case of Shawish' now famous all-diamond ring. The thrilling journey of crafting the most unique ring in the world was accomplished through passion and innovation. A ring made entirely of a faceted diamond has always been a fantasy for gemologists, but

N° 142

they are not usually the people designing
jewels. Mohamed Shawesh is a gemologist
and designer in one, so if it was up
to anyone to create this outrageously
ostentatious ring, it would need to be him.
The first great difficulty was finding a stone
big enough and of such a great quality
that one piece could be carved from it,
and be perfect from all angles. The risk
of the venture cannot be underestimated.
You cannot be sure that a stone of this size
is suitable for such a work of perfection.
There is also no certainty that the gem will

N° 143

N° 144

N° 145

N° 146

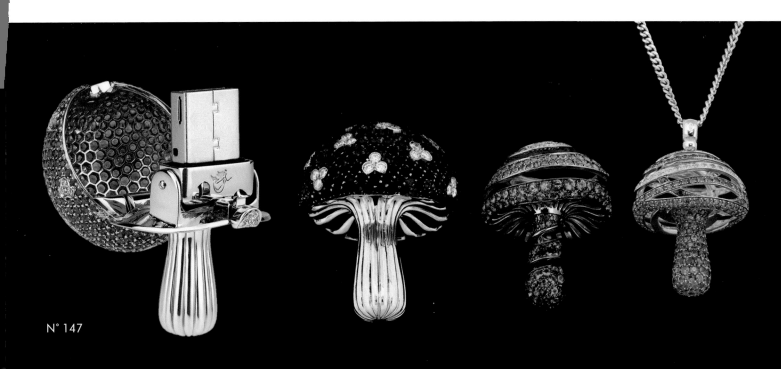

N° 147

not contain irregularities or imperfections, without cutting it first.

It took a team of specialists in the diamond world a year of hard work to examine the stone and experiment tirelessly to get the best angles and formulas for the finished gem. It was worth it. The cutting-edge laser technology was programmed specifically to cut miscellaneously into the 150 brut carat diamond. The final design of the ring is,

thus, one dictated by the needs of the stone, rather than a sketch by a jeweller.

The result has taken this fine creation past the boundaries of jewellery and into the realms of conceptual art. A celebration of nature, science and collective lapidary genius, the ring has already had hundreds of viewings with private collectors and will eventually be dispatched to one of them, after touring the world for other enthusiasts to gaze at in awe.

Who the ring will finally go to we cannot guess but it will not be hidden away in a secure vault. The ring, despite its curious premise, does in fact look marvellous on the finger - an additional surprise that amazed even the designer. What began as a technical experiment, ended with a genuinely beautiful creation.

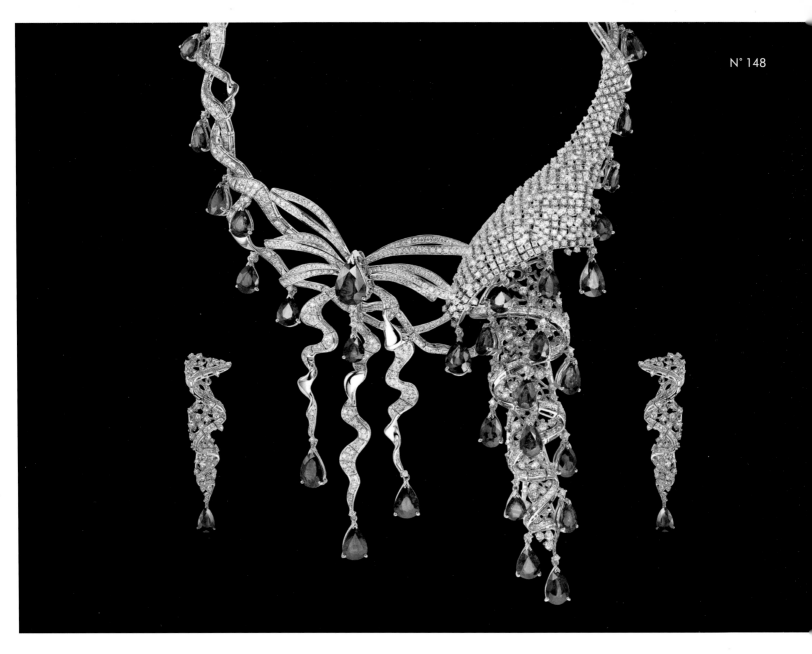

WALLACE CHAN

"I WANT TO CREATE DRAMATIC PIECES THAT NEVER CEASE TO AMAZE THE BEHOLDER."

WALLACE CHAN

A living master, Wallace Chan takes the term artist-jeweller to another level. Growing up in Hong Kong, Chan began his exotic journey into the world of Fine Jewellery design by training as a master carver of traditional Eastern *Objets d'Art*. Having mastered this revered skill, Chan travelled to Europe to learn how to create Italian *intaglio* carvings and cameos. In a deft move which has come to characterise Chan's work, he decided to combine both of these skills, harboured from both Eastern and Western ancient traditions, to invent something completely new. Inflating harmonius cameo iconography into three dimensional figures, he carved their visage into transparent blocks of stone. The effect is a ghostlike illusion that emanates an otherworldly energy - something which has become a standard in all Chan's work. Everyone who saw the creations was mystified by his raw talents both as a carver and as a technical innovator and considered him a genius in his

N° 150

field. Soon, Chan was getting commissions from the most discerning clients in the Far East, carving large-scale sculptures for revered Buddhist monasteries.
It was not long before the 'Michelangelo of the Orient' began experimenting with applying his artistry to Fine Jewellery.

While most jewellers are limited to setting their gems within a metal surround (using claws to hold their gems in place) Chan with his unique outlook as a carver and being familiar with the behaviour of solid stone, decided instead to set the stones inside one another, without using any metals as all.

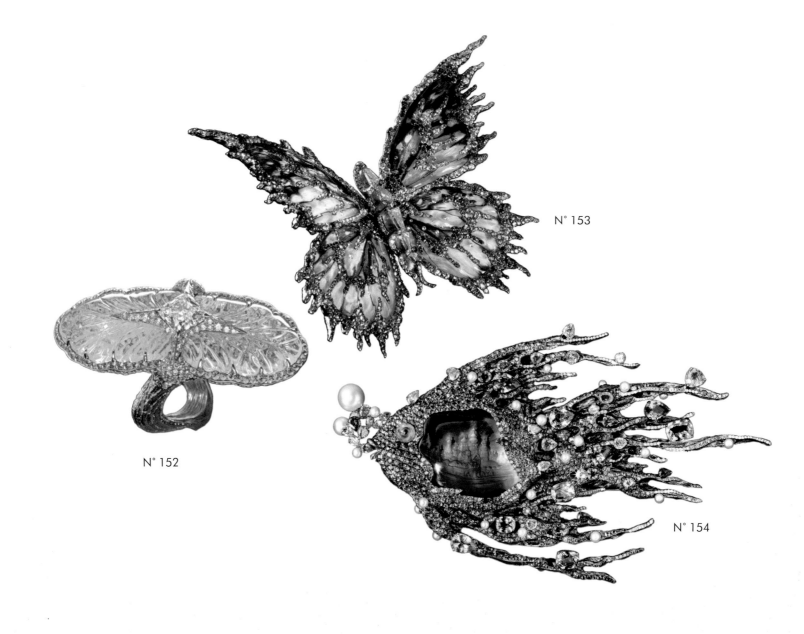

N° 153

N° 152

N° 154

Inspired by a method of joinery used in Ming-style architecture, Chan cut into the gems a mortise and tenon joint, so that they could fit together without any outside help. The results are magnificent. Brilliant white diamonds set directly into Jade, or nestled within a coloured opal; a giant ruby set flush inside a pearl. The gems did still need to be mounted, however. For this, the ever-demanding artist became enticed by the lightness of titanium and so began his eight-year trial of blending, casting and melting this challenging metal.

The wearable art jewels of Wallace Chan are the fruits of such intensive and extensive labour. Anyone lucky enough to behold such jewels in the flesh will be unable to describe in words what they have seen. The black opal fly, with its magical titanium frame and translucent wings looks like a magnified version of the genuine creature described in microscopic detail. When placed in the palm of the hand, it feels no heavier. It defies logic. Genius always does.

ZOLTAN DAVID

"FROM THE OLDER PRACTICES OF A TRADITIONAL ITALIAN JEWELLER TO A TRENDSETTING CONTEMPORARY DESIGNER. "

CHRISTIE'S

When an adventurous client approached Zoltan David with a 4 carat diamond and asked for it to be placed within an indestructible diamond ring, the Hungarian born designer barely flinched. *Dancing Metals Studio* is David's alchemist's laboratory for melting, welding, forging and inlaying metals and precious stones into other impossibly hard metals. David's work has not only garnered countless industry awards but leaves other jewellers scratching their heads: he's mastered the art of making the impossible, possible. His patented technique of 'shaped inlay' ornamentation displays an ability to create serious jewels, which can be worn every day. All fashioned by hand to the designer's exacting specifications; the innovative character and approach of this master of metals has made him the first port of call for jewels that can stand the test of time and that are resistant to an active, adventurous life. Using platinum as the metal of choice for many of his sculptural jewels means the work will retain the silky sheen this precious metal is

N° 156

known for. Where other jewellers are happy to settle for a simple metal design, David and his craftsmen go about inlaying the robust metal with beads of bright yellow gold, sparkling gems and diamonds of the highest grade. This demanding labour and intensive process is belied by the resulting jewel. Uncommonly pretty, the pieces glimmer and sparkle as innocently as objects conjured magically out of thin air. The delicacy of the jewels just takes the breath away, with the gold beading inlaid so seamlessly into the bed; it seems to have grown out of the white metal, like a flower sprouting from soil.

N° 159

N° 158

N° 160

This latest commission, however, demanded even more.

Already experimenting with black cobalt chromium, which is six times tougher than stainless steel, the artist suggested trying out the army grade material for the band of the ring. The metal has a diamond-like hardness and is the most resistant surface against scratching, denting and wear in all fine jewellery and timepieces. The next question for the designer would be how to penetrate a surface chosen for its impenetrability, for the sake of ornamenting it with gold and gems. Two and a half years after approaching this conundrum, there is a definite method to this master's madness. *The Knight Dreams* collection with its glossy black jewels, studded with yellow gold three-dimensional inlay and diamonds, is the result of this tireless work.

Strikingly contemporary in appearance, Zoltan David jewellery has an Old World philosophy behind it. For every jewel has been given individual attention; each piece is a phenomenon of metallurgy, craftsmanship and creative originality. The balance between the hard and soft metals, the warm yellow gold and black cobalt chromium or cold platinum, even the precious with the non-precious metals is what lies behind the artist's fascination with his artistic feats. His collectors appreciate the work he puts in and are open to pushing him further. Zoltan David and his team of alchemists welcome the challenge.

CARNET

"CARNET'S JEWELS DEMAND TO BE WORN TO BE APPRECIATED AS REMARKABLE OBJECTS OF BEAUTY."

ANONYMOUS COLLECTOR

The story of Carnet, from its inception in 1985 to the present day, demonstrates the full force of jewellery designer Michelle Ong's ever-evolving, charismatic and intuitive creativity, as it succeeds in transforming the jewel into a true work of art. Ong's jewellery takes form directly from what happens to inspire her; a spider's web, a single pear, a flower with petals curled just so, jewels of nature caught in a single moment. Sketches are then taken to her workshop where she and her craftsmen realise how to create the piece in order to capture the delicacy of her vision and remain artistically unfettered. The distinctive fusion of cultural influences from East and West, floating clouds, a Chinese dragon, magic hoops, jade carvings, an antique lace cuff, shimmering rose diamonds, chandelier earrings, are all resolutely contemporary, yet with emotive echoes of the past. The pieces show Ong's extraordinary use of colour, from brilliant to the most delicate shades, and her very particular gift for turning gems and metals into

N° 163

the lightest organdie or lace, trails of diamond-light that ripple around the neck, earrings that cascade with torrents of gems. Ong rarely creates her jewellery by commission. She says "The Carnet collector understands and appreciates that my work must be the perfect expression of the jeweller's art and the art of the jewel. For my collectors, every element works together to create something that exceeds the sum of its parts. They appreciate that my inspiration, my designs, my precious stones and materials, my technical

N° 164

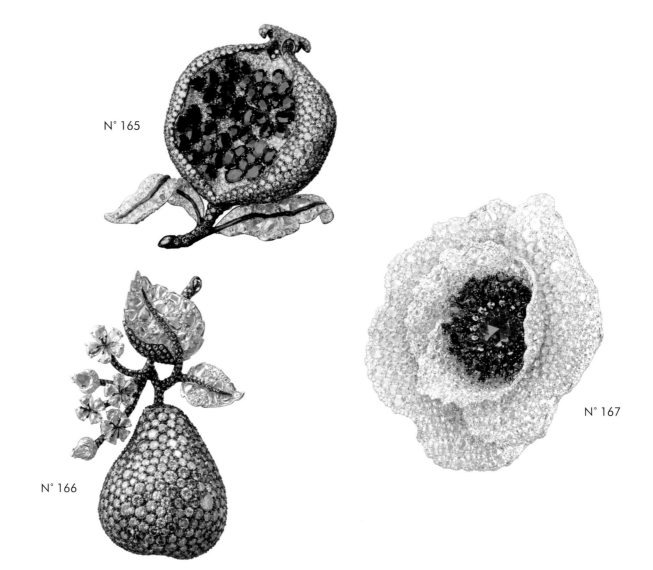

N° 165

N° 166

N° 167

demands all combine to hold a kind of 'magic' in the piece. For her *Dahlia* necklace, Ong visualised a mesmerising group of bejewelled flowers, clustered around the neck. Each flower has been created separately and then gathered together into a sumptuous garland. The flawless precious stones have been set in lightweight titanium, a metal which is difficult to work but wonderfully light for the wearer. As with all of Ong's pieces,

the back is as exquisite as the front, and the articulation is exceptionally intricate to ensure a perfect fit and comfort.

Crafted from one of nature's strongest metals, this effervescent necklace is interwoven as though it were a diaphanous lace scarf. Clinging to the neck like a scattering of damp petals, the flowers move and glitter as their multitudinous gems catch the light.

All of Michelle Ong's work meets the same standards. She is a contemporary designer who creates living, breathing jewels to match her own poetic vision of nature. That is why collectors stand in line to buy these Carnet jewels – pieces whose designs, craftsmanship and illimitable standards of perfection both belong to and enhance the story of High Jewellery across time.

FRANCIS MERTENS

"IT LOOKS EASY BUT YOU CANNOT COMPARE IT WITH OTHER, TRADITIONAL JEWELLERY."

FRANCIS MERTENS

Titanium is not classed as a precious metal. For most of us the high-tech metal conjures up images of space travel and dental surgery but for jewellers and designers who tolerate its stubborn nature, the most magnificent jewels can come from it. Lighter than aluminium but stronger than steel, the material allows jewels to be made on a far grander scale. Larger gems are supported safely with relatively little metal lending work futuristic appeal. The fact that titanium is so tough to work with has even made it a standard amongst high jewellers. Having no great history to weight it down, and no traditional techniques to draw on, the designers and craftsmen are left to create afresh whatever they can, through a process of painstaking repeated experimentation and practice. Mertens is able to bend this notoriously tough material to his will and he uses it in his work as it simply would not be possible to create from any other metal. The accuracy of his work designed using 3-D computer models relies on the unyielding

N° 169

strength of this metal to precisely contain its
intricate design.

His Japanese-inspired bonsai design
recalls a traditional silk painting. Barely an
ounce in weight, despite its 15 carats of
diamonds and tsavorites, the brooch is
impossibly delicate but as hardy as can be.
Oversized, open designs are also a signature
of Mertens as he designs razor thin lines

N° 170

N° 171

N° 172

N° 173

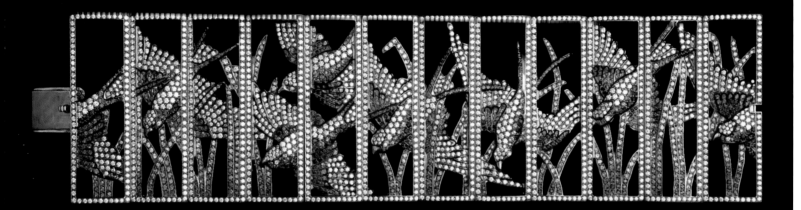

with the strength to form whatever shape he chooses. His tanzanite cuffs – designed to be worn as a pair - structurally mimic a pair of over-bleached formal shirt cuffs. Yet, the baroque openwork design within the body of the cuffs, embedded with 69 ct of diamonds throughout and 15 ct of tanzanite, is as elaborate as lace and looks as sharp as a knife's edge. The cuffs took a frustrating 4 months to perfect but perfection is the only standard Mertens adheres to.

The figurative element of the designer's work is something he loves to push to its limit. Taking full advantage of titanium's ability to turn all colours of the rainbow when oxidized, his metals can impersonate nature right down to gradations of tones, much like a painting. A brown twig, sprouting a single bud and leaf is so lifelike that, when worn as a brooch it imitates a sprig torn from a living plant and worn as a button hole.After decades of challenging designers and technicians, titanium has

finally met its match in Mertens. The result is a marriage of two uncompromising forces combining to create immeasurable beauty.

ONES TO
WATCH

ONES TO WATCH

LENA SKLYUT

"MY JEWELLERY IS FOR WOMEN…AWARE OF THEIR…STYLE…NOT PREOCCUPIED WITH FOLLOWING TRENDS."

LENA SKLYUT

Lena Sklyut's dramatic, oversized pieces are made to be noticed. Created in a rich, moody palette of dusky pinks and deep reds, the dark romanticism of the larger than life jewels are layered with imagery of snakes, flames, sea life and spiders' webs. Inspired by nature or Russian and French iconography, the sensuality of the work stands out particularly with outsized gems. The drama of these gargantuan stones is offset by prettiness in the palette and the temperament of the pieces, which ensures the jewels flatter and entice. In her *Spring* *Love* set inspired by the ocean, large Rose Quartz cabochons are set in textured yellow gold and encircled by small South Sea white pearls. Both the necklace and the ring from the set are poetically beautiful thanks to the size and presence of these large stones. A recent creation is a cuff and ring set inspired by a spider's web. Set with multicoloured tourmalines, the web is elaborately depicted in a yellow gold structure, which forms the solid cuff. One diamond encrusted spider, a ruby cabochon set on its back,

N° 175

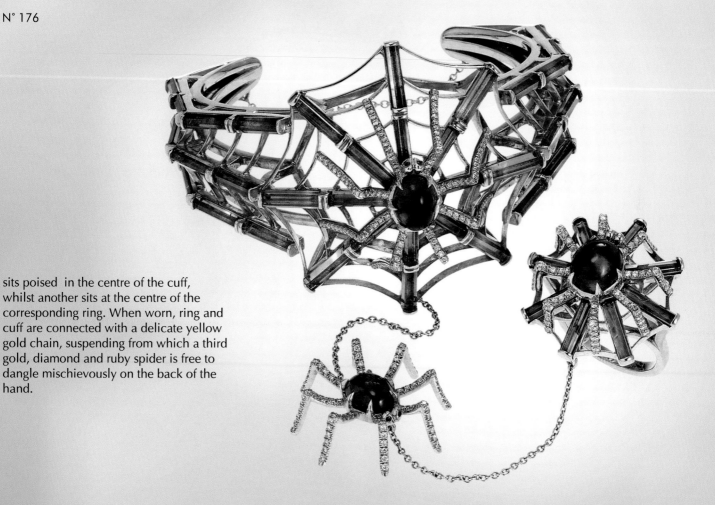

sits poised in the centre of the cuff, whilst another sits at the centre of the corresponding ring. When worn, ring and cuff are connected with a delicate yellow gold chain, suspending from which a third gold, diamond and ruby spider is free to dangle mischievously on the back of the hand.

NADA G

"I JUST LOVE THE GOOD ENERGY NADA'S PIECES HAVE; WEARING
THEM LIFTS ME UP."

NADA G COLLECTOR

Nada's travels with her family as a youngster inspired and fascinated her. Window displays around the world, opened her eyes to the core design elements she embraced in later life. Years later, her work in advertising helped her understanding of how to create and build her own brand. Yet, it was time spent with her grandmother and the sensational feeling derived from learning to weave pieces of art with her, that was the first shaping force in her life however. Nada G's jewels truly embody her life experiences and combine a human fragility with industrial strength. Nada G™ jewellery encapsulates the designer's world of experiences, showcasing intricate masterpieces that exhibit the designer's sense of order and form, designed as timeless pieces made of 18k gold and precious stones. Indeed, the black diamond *pavé* calligraphy detailing on her *Aya* rings appear to be precisely embroidered onto the side of the golden cages reminiscent of her first-ever collection, made from 18k golden string woven into wearable jewels. Her

N° 177

current collections emit the same energy of the artist-jeweller, with the immaculate finish of a high jewellery collection.

This Lebanese designer attracts clients and faithful collectors worldwide, notably younger clients who love her fresh, architectural designs and her reinterpretations of precious gold and diamonds for a new generation.

N° 178

SARAH HO

Sarah Ho was raised by Fine Jewellery Collectors. In particular, her grandmother Clementina; a fine lady from Macau who would not dream of taking tea without her magnificent jewels, and of course in full make-up. It is this lost world of glamour and elegance that Sarah's magical pieces are able to capture, but with a fashionable, contemporary edge. A vintage piece which Sarah inherited from Clementina -a gold pendant with jade and diamonds- has been taken by the designer as a key influence in her aptly named Clementina rings, which boldly mix stones such as Tiger's Eye, Lapis Lazuli and Aventurine with diamonds, pink sapphires and yellow gold. In part due to her training in fashion design at the London College of Fashion, Ho is able to take even the most classical styles and give them a youthful, cutting-edge feel, without following trends or seasonal fashions. In particular, her *origami* rings in which gold is folded like Japanese paper art to create a flat-topped ring, exposing pearls and gems, are witty and conceptual but with such

N° 179

delicacy and polish that they will remain design classics for future generations. Now that Ho's collectors have evolved, in particular her bespoke clients, she has also progressed to her first Couture line. Giant colourful stones appear to hang from dainty *pavé*-studded gold swirls in these beautiful creations. Ho's signature fastidious attention to detail and her organic shapes complement the pastel tones in the romantic collection, making them ripe for a lover of timeless jewels.

SHARON KHAZZAM

"I HOPE TO PASS DOWN THESE JEWELS TO MY FAMILY, GIVING
THEM A GLIMPSE OF WHO I AM."

ANONYMOUS COLLECTOR

After training at New York City's Fashion Institute of Technology, Sharon Khazzam was instantly singled out as a young talent ripe for nurturing by the traditional English jewellery house Asprey. It was then that she was given the opportunity of a lifetime. She was sent to be apprenticed to the great master jeweller Carvin French, who has created some of the finest high jewellery pieces for the great Parisian *Maisons* over the last few decades. By the time Sharon had launched her own collection years later, she had mastered the art of using her great knowledge of gems and goldsmiths' techniques to break as many of these rules as she could. She created unusual and enigmatic pieces that collectors had never seen anywhere else. Her *Mosaic Cuff* is characteristic of the designer's aesthetic. It consists of 434 stones all varying in size, shape, colour, tone and cut residing together in harmony on a nearly invisible golden cage cuff. Amazingly, the designer has even mixed cabochons with faceted stones, a definite departure from the rules of

N° 181

classical fine jewellery. Despite the random appearance of the bracelet, it works precisely because every stone has been meticulously set in the correct colour of gold to suit its tone and pieced together like a puzzle to create this exquisite stained glass effect.

This technical masterpiece is just one of Khazzam's unique jewels, which are as free in spirit as the designers and her collectors.

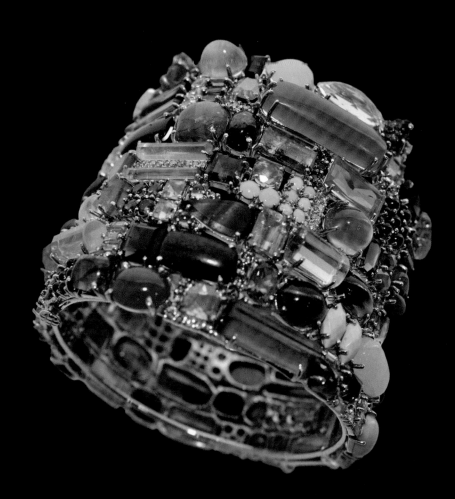

SPECIAL
SECTION

YVES FREY

An Insight

N° 183

YVES FREY

DIAMONDS

Antwerp is one of the most important diamond centres in the world, not just for merchants, but also for polishers and stonecutters.

I was born into the fourth generation of an Antwerp diamond merchant family. Some may say that it was inevitable I should become an expert in these beautiful stones. Others may assume that growing up surrounded by these stunning, sparkling and magical gems, I would be instantly drawn into the family business. After all, who would not want to be surrounded by such beauty all day, every day?

In fact, I had little interest in being a diamond dealer myself, or a jewellery designer, as I was growing up. I wanted, more than anything, to travel and see the world, to experience life outside Antwerp and the industry. My first major career decision was to go to Paris. It was there that I discovered the work of the great philanthropic banker Albert Kahn. He sent photographers all over the world, commissioning them to document their journeys through photography and film, still a new art form at the time. Seeing these images gave me a taste for exploration, for seeing

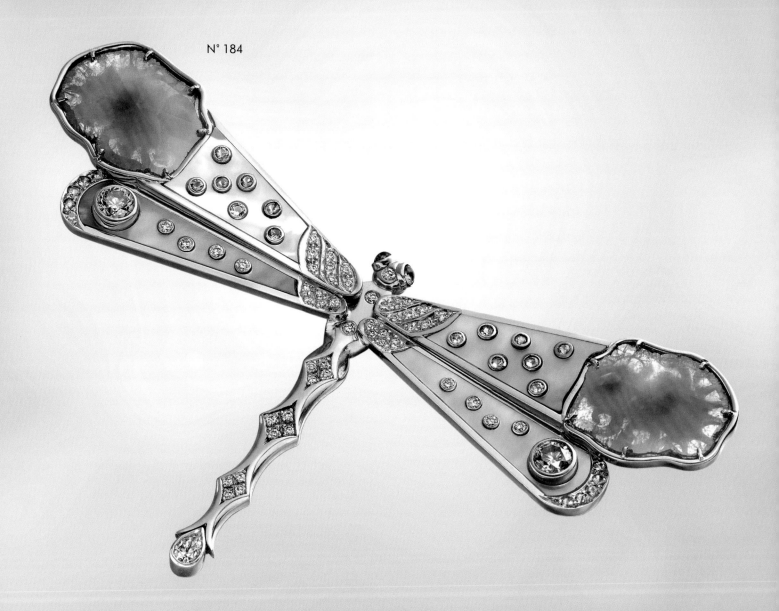

N° 185

new horizons and experiencing as much as I could during my own lifetime. Like Kahn, I began working in banking, and, like him, I took time out to travel the rest of the world. It was as magnificent as I had imagined, and as important in developing my own creative vision as any formal training in the arts. It was through my work as a banker that I ended up stationed in London. Hatton Garden was thriving as a centre for gems, in particular, high quality jewellery production and also, of course, diamonds. My family was, at this time, incorporating natural fancy coloured diamonds into their business. Perhaps, rather hesitantly, I was gently persuaded to revisit diamonds, as a possible interest, even a career. It was at this point that the wonder of colour diamonds

worked their magic on me. Diamonds come in every shade conceivable. It is nature at its most varied, most exquisite. The sparkle of a well cut stone and the way in which light is channelled through a fancy coloured diamond produces a magical effect. A stone can reflect memories of your life which are personal to you.

This is why people keep coming back to diamonds over and over again throughout history. It is why I came back to them. Having seen the world, I had now so many visual experiences to draw on, that each stone meant something to me, which it would not have done when I was younger. The stones also enhance your experiences. Of all the diamonds I have seen in my own life, my favourite

N° 186

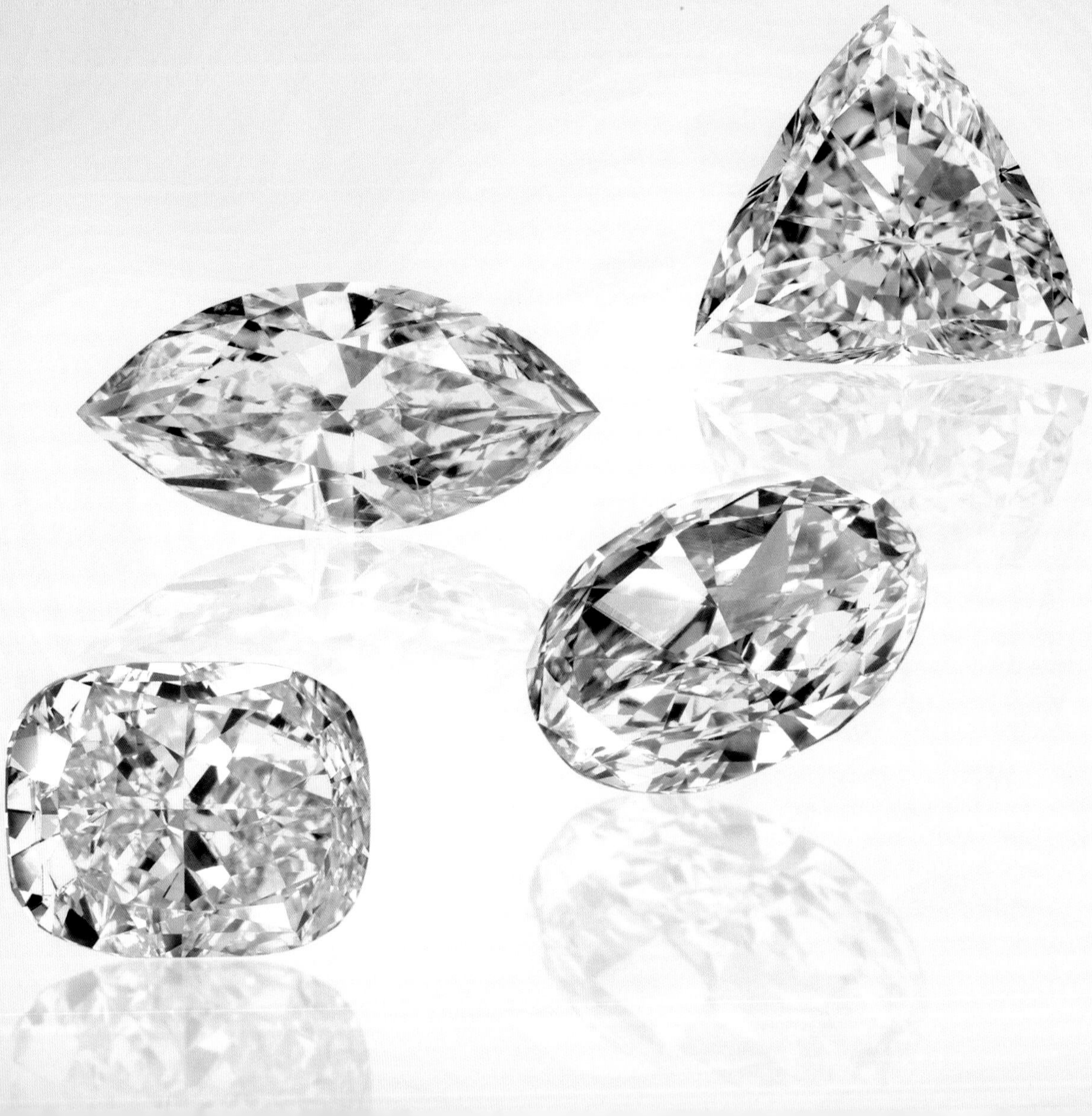

N° 187

N° 188

was a deep, flame orange colour. When I looked at it through my loupe, the tangerine tones became emblazoned on my brain. I have never looked at a tangerine in the same way again. Nor have they ever tasted better to me, since feasting my eyes on that stone.

It is not always the rarest or the most expensive stone which captures the imagination. For example the rarest and most expensive diamond is the natural fancy red. I have seen just one such stone and found it to be truly magnificent. Equally magnificent is the stone that captures someone's heart when they first lay eyes on it. I have many people come into my offices in Hatton Garden to look at my collection of natural fancy coloured diamonds. The process is so deeply personal, that I can never tell exactly what people will want just by speaking to them, or asking questions. The only way to find someone's perfect stone is to place the gems in front of them, allow them to reach instinctively for the one which catches their eye and then place the gem loose between their fingers. I wait for a certain look in their eye, a barely visible expression, but one which is unmistakable. Then I know that they have found their stone. Sometimes, they do not even know what they are looking for themselves. I recently had a lady visit me who claimed she was not hugely fond of diamonds. She simply did not understand why everyone was so obsessed with the stone. I placed a few trays in front of her and then

N° 189

N° 190

heard her gasp and exclaim, "What stone is that?" It was a deep steely grey oval cut diamond. She did not even know a diamond could be such a colour. I pulled the stone out and placed it lightly on her hand, under a bright light and let the stone enchant her. At that moment she was converted to diamonds. She was with me in the office for two more hours, looking at the stone next to brilliant whites, which bring out the depth of the grey and in different lights to see the way the stone changes in every environment. This is pretty typical for an experience with a new client. Over time, clients come back to me and they become increasingly attuned to the different qualities of a stone. They start to notice the way colour responds to different polishing techniques and they get a very

strong sense of what they like. People associate diamonds mostly with jewellery, but many collectors are simply gem enthusiasts. They begin by being enchanted by the earth's minerals. If you continue to be interested in stones long enough, it is inevitable that you will end up gazing into a diamond. It is one of earth's greatest phenomena.

People are deeply comforted by the fact that the stones are billions of years old. When our own lives are so fleeting, to hold something in your hand which took millions of years to form and which is as unique as a fingerprint, is deeply moving.
It is also astonishing to think that something which comes from so deep in the earth's core can explode

and come to life under the light of the sun. I have spent decades looking deep into these stones under bright light, and I am still humbled by them. I find that everyone who wears a diamond finds some kind of spiritual connection with it. I see a woman wearing a diamond ring that has been on her finger for decades, still looking at it and watching it sparkle in the sunlight when she has a quiet moment to think. A good diamond has therapeutic qualities, in that sense. These are the treasures I travel the world looking for now, for my private clients.

One of my greatest pleasures is receiving newly engaged couples. People need that trust at this moment in their lives. It's the first outing they take together in life, before they start the whole wedding process. Helping them create something beautiful and unique is a process I never tire of, despite the work involved. I continue to see them throughout their lives. Rarely do people only come to have a piece made from me once. They return whenever something in their lives deserves commemorating. Over time, I get a sense of their tastes. Getting that connection with a client is essential to me.
The reason I became a designer of jewellery was not

to go into retail. It was an organic development, as every diamond needs to have a particular setting. Just like every person suits different clothing and cosmetics, so, too do these gems need to be dressed to their best. I begin with placing the stone along with other stones which may compliment it. It is a time consuming, but vital process. Then, I work with a detailed sketch, taking into account the best angle at which the stone should sit, the level of its exposure, the colour and design of the setting and also where the piece will be worn. I always take into account how a person moves, how they live and how they wear their jewels. The jewellery needs to compliment them and their lives. That is how my collections of stackable delicate rings were created.

More and more clients wanted rings that they could wear every day, or rings of different colours to match various moods, or stacked up on one another.
So *Les Adorables* and then *Les Mini Adorables* were conceived. I find that people love to give them to their daughters, for various achievements. As the daughters get older, the rings stack up and I know that they will then pass them on to the next generation.
Diamonds are, after all, timeless.

HERITAGE

Siegelson N.Y.

N° 192

HERITAGE
SIEGELSON N.Y.

Third-generation gem and jewellery dealer Lee Siegelson is president and owner of Siegelson, New York.

Established in 1920, the renowned company is recognized by museum curators, magazine editors, and jewellery houses as a leading source of and authority on rare jewellery, gemstones, and objects of art. Lee joined the company in 1992, and took over the business two years later when his father died. The company now deals exclusively with the best examples of fine gemstones and diamonds, antique and estate jewellery, objects of art, contemporary designers, and jewellery by Siegelson.

For hundreds of years people have been interested in buying and selling jewellery and in the last two decades, the public has gained knowledge through major museum exhibitions on the likes of Cartier and Van Cleef & Arpels, and through topics like Art Deco. Museums are showing an interest in works of great design and Siegelson avidly supports museum exhibitions lending to more than 15 of them in the past five years. The Egyptian-inspired scarab buckle

was a keynote jewel selected for the exhibition Cartier and America held at the Legion of Honor, Fine Arts Museums of San Francisco, while the diamond Vanderbilt Rose brooch was featured in The Nature of Diamonds at the Royal Ontario Museum in Toronto, the Houston Museum of Natural Science, and The Field Museum in Chicago.

The Duke and Duchess of Windsor were renowned collectors whose collection reflects their ideas about art. The blue chalcedony suite by Suzanne Belperron echoes the couple's astute and stylish taste. Belperron was a wonderfully artful designer who had been forgotten until the famous 1987 sale of the Duchess of Windsor's jewellery. A collector should find the area they are drawn to, educate themselves through some of the excellent publications and museum

exhibitions available, and purchase the best examples of design they can find. Some of the names to look for today include the well-known firms of Cartier, Castellani, Van Cleef & Arpels, and Boucheron but also lesser-known, forgotten, or more artistic firms, such as Maison Boivin, Suzanne Belperron, Paul Flato, Marcus & Co., Raymond Templier, and Maison Fouquet. The most magnificent examples of design are increasingly hard to find. Ultimately, the collector should find a firm or dealer that has the knowledge and taste they feel confident in. A quality dealer will have connections to find great pieces and the knowledge to help the collector make the best decision.

GEMFIELDS

Coloured Stones

N° 195

GEMFIELDS
COLOURED STONES

The ethical mining of the world's finest, precious coloured gems.

Emeralds - The mysterious deep green emerald is one of the most prized coloured gemstones on Earth. The most valuable of the Beryl group, emeralds are not easily categorised by conventional standards due to their unique characteristics and rare qualities. Although highly-saturated colours and inclusion-free gems are extremely rare and most precious, the unique identification of an emerald's jardins, or inclusions, can often contribute to its allure.

The main emerald-producing countries are Zambia, Columbia and Brazil. Physically, Zambian emeralds range in colour from a natural, rich saturated green to a vibrant green with slight bluish undertones. Although less common than gemstones from Colombia, Zambian emeralds are available at significantly lower prices, opening up the market to new customers looking for beautiful gems at a spectacular value. Zambian emeralds mined by Gemfields are unique in several other regards. Gemfields has created the

N° 197

N° 198

world's first integrated pipeline to bring emeralds directly from the mine to the international market. This means that consumers will now be able to trace the origin of each gem from the source and can follow its journey to purchase. With the democratically-elected Government of the Republic of Zambia as part-owners, Gemfields produces approximately 20% of the world's emerald supply, which is renowned for a rich, deep colour and superior quality. This state-of-the-art mining facility is able to produce a reliable and consistent conflict-free emerald supply from a responsible source.

The history of emeralds is long and prolific; in fact, records show that the gem was bought and sold in

Babylonian markets as early as 4000 BC. Egyptian Queen Cleopatra is possibly the most famous admirer of emeralds, and her own mine was rediscovered a century ago – one of the earliest confirmations of emeralds in history. Even ancient Western literature contains references to these rare stones: Aristotle wrote that owning an emerald would help the wearer with victory in trials, settling litigation, success in business matters and even with poor eyesight.

Later, emeralds were highly prized by the Incas and Aztecs when discovered in Colombia. Many other cultures have embraced emeralds as their own, and ascribe much value to the green gems. Whether a centerpiece of Russian crown jewels, part of a collection of the Iranian State Treasure, or a favourite of Indian Shahs, emeralds have long been associated with royalty and status. Shah Jahan of India, famous for building the Taj Mahal, was so enamoured by emeralds that he inscribed his collection with sacred texts and used them as talismans.

There is no doubt that emeralds have always been valued for their mythological powers and strengths. The gem was commonly known to help and soothe

vision (Nero was said to view gladiator fights through a large, transparent emerald), and the colour green has always had an association with spring and rebirth. In fact, ancient Egyptians often buried mummies with an emerald hung from their neck in hopes of providing eternal youth.

Many physical and emotional ailments are also said to be helped by wearing emeralds. Throughout time, these gems have been assigned healing powers for: depression, insomnia, the immune system, diabetes and blood detoxification, among many others. As if that wasn't enough, emeralds are also associated with love, fidelity, inspiration, wisdom, harmony, growth, patience, peace and abundance.

Amethysts - The divine deep purple of amethyst has for generations been regarded as source of inspiration. The most vibrant of the Quartz group, amethysts are characterised by their availability of larger crystals, the opportunity for artistic faceting interpretations and exceptionally intense colour.

The main amethyst producing countries are Zambia, Brazil, Bolivia and Uruguay. Zambia particularly is a

N° 200

major source of gemstones for the world's jewellery market. It offers some of the best amethysts in the world.

African Amethyst is praised for its colour and quality. The colour of an African amethyst is richer and deeper than that of amethysts from other origins. Highly-saturated colours and inclusion-free gems are extremely rare and most precious. African amethysts can be found in a wide range of purple shades – a deep violet with red or blue flashes being the most valuable variety.

Throughout time, amethyst has been the stone of spirituality and contentment revealing the ultimate nature and meaning of life to those willing to discover it. Bishops, kings and scientists referred to amethyst as a source of spiritual enrichment.

Amethyst is one of the oldest known gemstones. Discovered in approximately 3100 BC in Egypt, it was used in jewellery and seal making by the Egyptians and Greeks. Cleopatra's signet ring of amethyst was engraved with a figure of the Persian God of 'The Divine Idea', a source of inspiration and spirituality.

In Europe, amethyst was recognised as the gemstone of high clergy and royalty. Its majestic purple colour and purity of hue signified the wine transformed to Christ's blood in the sacrament of the Mass. The signature stone of bishops, amethyst was used to fashion goblets for important spiritual celebrations. Royal jewellery collections of the British, Russian and Scandinavian ruling dynasties include amethyst masterpieces. In Asia, amethyst is associated with Buddha. Marvellous amethyst rosaries have been created there to promote clarity of mind and tranquillity.

OCTIUM

Boutique Luxury

N° 201

OCTIUM
BOUTIQUE LUXURY

Inspired by her mother's love of fine jewels and diamonds, Alanood Al Sabah's appreciation of the intricacies of jewellery design began when she was young.

When at college, her interest developed into a passion, as she indulged in sketching jewellery designs in her spare time whilst studying for her degree in architecture. For Al Sabah, jewellery is art in its most luxurious form; in her view, timeless pieces like the ones in her collection are an investment for the future, as you transfer them onto younger generations.

In 2009, with the help of her husband Fahad Al Hajiri, she decided to share her talent and passion with the world, and the couple established their own luxury brand, Octium in their native Kuwait. The creative and dynamic pair divide their workload according to their talents; Al Hajiri is responsible for the business side of the company, while Al Sabah steers the design department. They are zealous travellers, and they draw on their experiences as inspiration for their work. The name Octium is inspired by the number 8, which in many cultures across the world is a symbol for happiness, prosperity

N° 202

N° 203

and good fortune. The cyclical nature of the figure 8 itself promotes the idea of an endless quest for excellence, which suits the ethos of Al Sabah's brand completely. The design of the jewellery is centralized around this idea, and the brand's creations succeed in epitomizing the couples' passion for precision and perfection.

Al Sabah, while being an enthusiastic designer of jewellery, is also a keen collector. It had always been the dream of this visionary pair to one day create a line of jewellery, but they first wanted to establish their boutique as a place where other jewellers could display their work. They did this with the creation of their own multi-brand jewellery store. Al Sabah

is a connoisseur of the field and prides herself on her interest in local and lesser-known jewellers, not just the iconic, popular brands (although she adores Buccellati for their craftsmanship). As a result of her travels, Al Sabah believes there to be glimmers of talent in all corners of the globe and she strives to demonstrate this as much as possible in her collection. In her admiration and presentation of the work of these lesser-known designers, she succeeds in promoting and nurturing their creativity, which would otherwise have gone undetected. The couple have good relationships with all of their designers, and endeavour to transport their designs to the Middle East, where tastes are exponentially more varied than people are lead to believe. Prominent independent jewellers have

N° 204

N° 205

claimed that they are sought-after by collectors in the Middle East and it is this idea that prompted Al Sabah and her husband to create their shop, so that designers might be provided with the opportunity to present their collections to a new market. Al Sabah also wished to use her space to create an Art Gallery for jewels, a place where aesthetics and creativity collide to create a unique display; in short it is a veritable treasure trove.

With their boutique causing a stir both nationally and internationally, Al Sabah took the opportunity to step into the arena of design herself and create her own collection, entitled Octium Creates: Series One. The result of Alanood's decision to unleash

her creativity onto the world was an excellent one. Her penchant for all things bright and beautiful is blissfully evident in her work, and as a result Octium is set to make a big impression on the Kuwaiti and international jewellery market. Her passion for opulence and luxury is abundant in her designs, and as a result the brand has achieved the remarkable feat of being the first and only Kuwaiti jewellery brand to debut its Series One collection to appear during Paris Fashion Week and in Harrods department store in London. The collection debuted at the 360 Mall at the Octium Boutique in December 2011. The pieces within the collection are designed with the number 8 in mind; each one is a variation of the tilted octagonal shape, which links in perfectly with the philosophy

N° 206

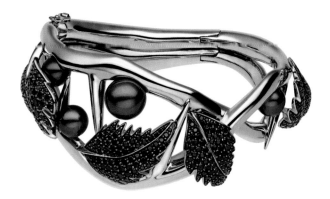

N° 207

behind the company's name. The jewellery is both cast and fabricated in 18k rose gold and set with dazzling diamonds. This combination results in a series of designs that are breathtaking. Upon the success of their debut, the couple are planning on second, third and fourth collections. The future collections will feature yellow and white gold, with the introduction of colour coming in later. They strive to create a sense of character and identity for each stone, so that each piece evokes individual charm. The design process is infinite, as the team endeavour to create an object of perfection, a piece of which they can all be proud. The initial design process is a special period for the couple, as they devote themselves entirely to the development of their creations. The primary sketches are reviewed

by the couple before anyone else has any input, so that they can deliberate over which designs truly represent them. The designs are then handed over to their in-house jewellery designer who is responsible for manufacturing the individual pieces; this is performed under supervision by the couple as the designs are constantly evolving throughout this process.

The pair plan to have their future collections featured in the most prestigious boutiques and department stores around the globe. They aim ultimately to establish Octium as an international luxury lifestyle brand.

MIKIMOTO

Pearls

N° 208

MIKIMOTO
PEARLS

The originator of cultured Pearls since 1893

Mr. Mikimoto, was the first to develop a technique for the cultivation of pearls including Japanese Akoya pearls, South Sea pearls from Australia, Indonesia and The Philippines and black pearls from Tahiti. The family-run business remains the world leader in superior-quality Akoya and South Sea cultured pearls and is internationally respected for its product design, crafting techniques and strict quality control.

After discovering the pearl cultivation process in 1893, Mr. Mikimoto was granted a patent by the Japanese government in 1896. He sent artisans to Europe to master the techniques of jewellery production and design and in 1899, equipped with his first collection, Mr. Mikimoto opened the first Mikimoto Pearl Store in Tokyo. After improving his cultivating and harvesting techniques, Mr. Mikimoto was able to ship his product overseas, making cultured pearls one of the first successful export products for Japan. Over a century after their discovery, Mikimoto

cultured pearls are still grown in the vast, world-renowned pearl farms of Ago Bay, Japan.

Pearls are formed naturally when an intrusion such as a shell fragment or grain of sand, lodges inside the oyster's shell. The oyster surrounds this irritant with a protective veil of calcium carbonate, called nacre, to form a pearl. The process of cultivating pearls mimics nature's process. A nucleus, made of pig-toe shell, is manually inserted into only the healthiest oysters. This process is what distinguishes a cultured pearl from a natural pearl. When the oysters are returned to the sea in wire mesh baskets, nature takes over, coating the nucleus with pearly layers of nacre. About half of all the pearls harvested in Japan are approved for export. Of these, only a small percentage meet Mikimoto's exclusive standard of excellence. Mikimoto has been grading its pearl quality since 1974 with a unique system based on the lustre, colour, shape and surface perfection of each pearl.

Lustre: The surface glow and the way light refracts off the pearl.
Colour: The spectrum of colours in pearls is vast. Colour should be rich and even.
Shape: Perfectly round pearls are rarest and most valuable.
Surface: Tiny marks are part of a pearl's natural texture. However, the cleaner the pearl, the higher its value.

Before Mr. Mikimoto developed the method of culturing a spherical pearl, all pearls were naturally irregular in shape. A perfectly spherical, lustrous pearl was extremely rare; therefore, pearls became as expensive as diamonds. Mr. Mikimoto's success made them more accessible to the public, creating an entire industry.

PRECIOUS METALS

Elemental

PRECIOUS METALS

ELEMENTAL

The story of gold is intimately intertwined with that of Fine Jewellery.

Any question as to which takes precedence - the currency value of the glittering metal or its beauty - is futile. Gold is an adornment used as a sign of wealth, eminence and power that has been a constant in every culture since time began.

Herein lays the secret of gold. Its constant metamorphosis into countless forms, from solid sculptures through to the most delicate thread (while retaining its lustre), means it can perform in many ways. Clothing and tapestries can be woven and embroidered entirely from gold; homes and statues can be plated with it. Gold leaf can even be used to garnish gourmet ice-cream.

To add flamboyance or divine significance to any ambience, person or place, gold sets the standard. Naturally, its warm and yellow tones have long been associated with the sun. The most powerful men and women in history, including Cleopatra, Alexander the

N° 212

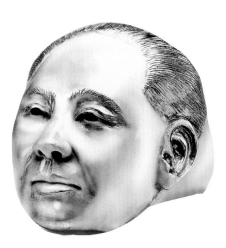

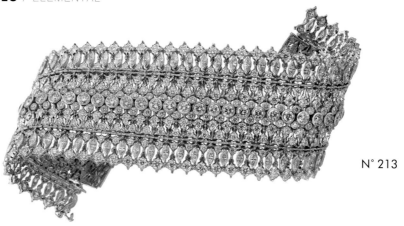

N° 213

Great and Louis XIV the Sun King are usually depicted as 'golden' icons. For most jewellers, though, choosing gold as a working material has little to do with its market value or precious quality. Jewellers and designers tend to use gold because of the pleasure derived from working with it. The pliability of this precious metal allows for the creation of nearly any jewel imaginable. When stuck for creative ideas, jewellers can draw from thousands of years' worth of goldsmiths' techniques for inspiration.

A case in point is the Italian house of Buccellati whose textured gold techniques date back to the Renaissance. Using methods known as Rigato, Telato and Segrinato on the surface of their signature gold cuffs,

they are able to engrave a variety of textures onto the gold, so that it appears to have been spun or tightly woven from the finest gold thread. Their engraving and openwork is the most labour intensive. Gold is transformed into intricate lace by the hands of master goldsmiths. Buccellati have built a loyal following precisely because of the time put into the work and the scarcity of the goldsmiths who have the necessary skills to work with such techniques. In an age of mass production, these are far more precious than the metal itself.

Cutting-edge designers also love to play with gold. Theo Fennell's ironic Heroes and Villains ring collection revels in the gaucheness of the solid yellow gold,

N° 215

which at times has been tarnished by its association with gross ostentation.

Nicholas Varney has also used a dental drill to engrave a baroque design onto the surface of a solid gold cuff, whilst Lorenz Bäumer likes to play with a variety of golden colours, from white and yellow to rose and brown gold. Because this chameleon-like metal can change its colour so readily, it is able to flatter the colour of every gemstone as well as any skin tone. Unfortunately, alongside its beauty and precious quality, comes a temperamental streak. Gold lacks the strength and the constancy of platinum, which is a far harder metal, less prone to scratching and denting. For setting diamonds, platinum is considered to be a wiser choice, as the stone cannot break free so easily from the claws of this metal. With its bright white sheen and its refusal to fade, corrode or oxidise, platinum also outshines gold in the preciousness and rarity stakes.

Somehow, the difficulty of working with a tougher metal is as much of a draw to some designers as it is a drawback for others. Cartier was a major pioneer in the use of platinum in the early 20th century, and many of the pieces from that period are still in the same perfect condition now as they were then. Jewellers love to create jewels which will one day become heirlooms. Platinum, like a diamond, is forever. Of course, there are a growing number of High Jewel-

N° 216

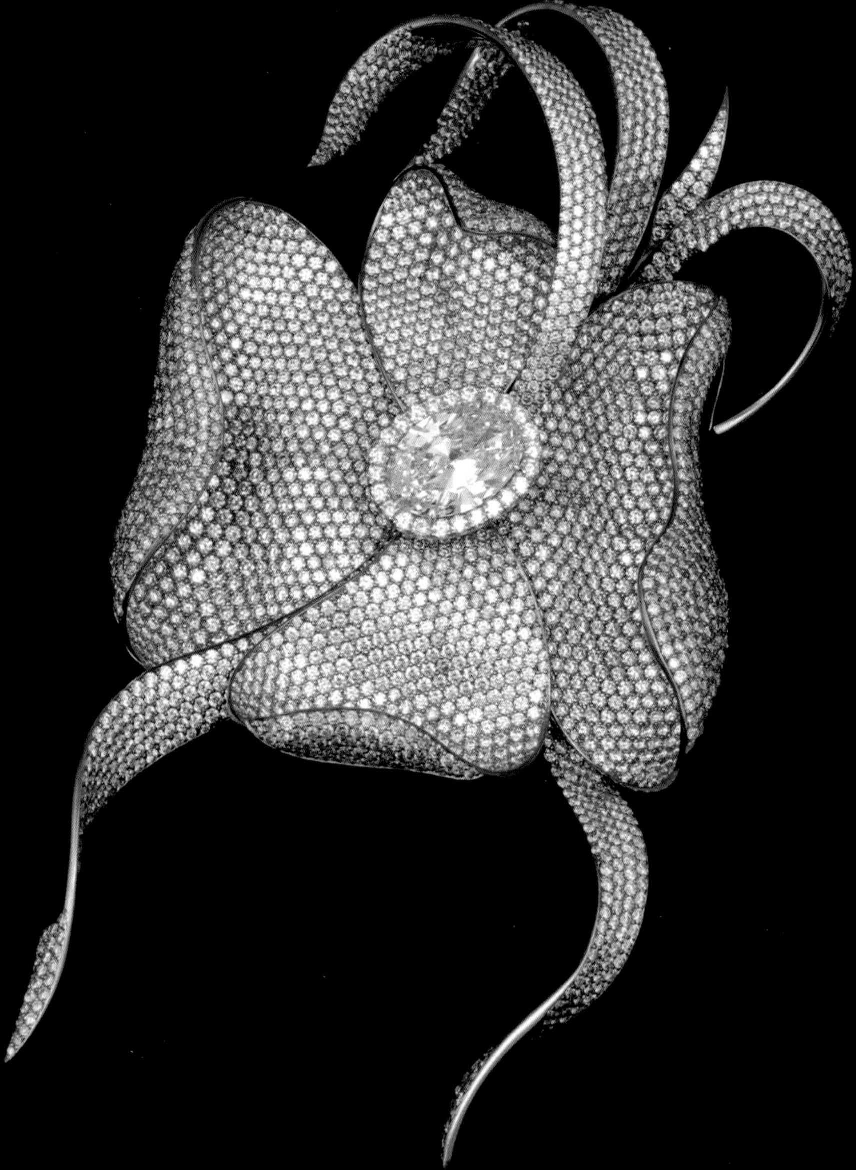

N° 217

N° 218

lers who are not limited to precious metals to create something magnificent.

Zoltan David's pioneering Knight Dreams collection is forged out of Cobalt Chromium, a glossy black metal, which has not been oxidized to obtain its darkened surface and so will retain its colour forever. David's collections are indefatigable and boast industry strength. They are also embedded with gold and diamonds, making this one of the New Age jewellers who is happy to mix precious materials with other metals.

Titanium is a particularly popular material for jewellers who have the skill to manipulate it. Strong but

weightless, it is the new age metal, allowing jewels to defy gravity, supporting giant stones on near invisible settings. When made visible, the metal can also be made to look delightfully pretty, in magical hues of blue, pink and dusky gold. Any metal can win a supporting role in a piece of Fine Jewellery. Fabio Salini has been experimenting with green, oxidized copper whilst the ultra-exclusive Paris based Jeweller JAR has used aluminium in his precious creations.

So long as it is in the right hands, even the basest of metals can be part of a precious masterpiece.

Index & Appendix

A™

Alexandra Mor™
New York

BOUCHERON
PARIS

BUCCELLATI®

BVLGARI

CARTIER

143-144 Sloane Street
London, SW1X 9AY
UK
Tel +44 (0)20 7312 6920
cuk.sloane@cartier.com

IMAGE DESCRIPTION

20. *Art Moderne Silver, Gold and and Sapphire Cuff, circa 1940 (Lee Siegelson Collection)*
21. *Art Moderne Gold, Citrine and Diamond Suite, circa 1938 (Lee Siegelson Collection)*

CHOPARD

12 New Bond Street
London, W1S 3SS
UK
Tel +44 (0)20 7409 3140
boutique.london@chopard.co.uk

IMAGE DESCRIPTION

22. *Apple Diamond Ring*
23. *High Jewellery Flower Necklace*

Chopard

CINDY CHAO

The Art Jewel
Beijing, Hong Kong
New York
Taiwan
info@cindychao.com

IMAGE DESCRIPTION

80. *Odyssey Earring*
81. *Royal Butterfly*
82. *Emerald City Ring*
83. *Solstice Cuff*
84. *Flames Earrings (front and back)*
85. *Equinox Cuff*

CINDY CHAO
THE ART JEWEL

FABERGÉ

FABERGE.COM

IMAGE DESCRIPTION

24. *Ruban de la Rose Ring*
25. *Le Collier Délices d'Été*
26. *Charmeuse Pink and White Ring*
27. *Katharina Earrings*
28. *White Hibiscus cuff*
29. *Oeuf Matelassé Empereur Diamants Or Blanc*
30. *Oeuf Or Blanc Spirale*

FABERGÉ

FABIO SALINI

Via di Monserrato 18
Rome, 00186, Italy
Tel +39 06 68301172
info@fabiosalini.it
FABIOSALINI.COM

IMAGE DESCRIPTION

86. *Titanium Bracelet with Green Tourmalines and Diamonds*
87. *Stingray necklace with diamonds and rubies*
88. *Venus Necklace*
89. *Ebony wood bracelet and fancy diamonds*
90. *Leather Ring and Diamonds*
91. *Ruban Earrings with White and Yellow Diamonds*
92. *Sapphire, Diamond and Titanium bracelet*
93. *The Enchanted Garden Necklace*
94. *Galuchat and Ruby Necklaces, Contraire Ring in Diamond and Ruby, Bow Ring in Diamond and Ruby*
95. *Anemone Titanium Earrings, Catena Ring with Diamonds and Ruby, Titanium and Rubellite Drop Earrings, Pink Titanium and Rubellite Earrings*

FABIO SALINI

FARAH KHAN

Tel +91 66149000

info@farahkhan.net

Image Description

37. *Tanzanite, Emerald and Diamond Mystique Bracelet*
38. *Social Butterfly Brooch*
39. *Cascades for waves ring with a lemon topaz in the centre with diamonds*
40. *Green grandeur butterfly ring*
41. *Royal rhapsody peacock cuff*
42. *An evening in Paris bow necklace*
43. *Regalia blue tanzanite and yellow diamond earrings.*
44. *Vanity Fair 3 faced ring*
45. *Swanlake swan ring*
46. *Eve's garden cuff*
47. *Mughal Ancestry pearl and ruby earrings*

FRANCIS MERTENS

Antwerp

Belgium

Tel +32(0)3 222.93.02

Info001@idhtitanium.com

idhtitanium.com

Image Description

169. *Titanium Ruby and Rubellite cuff*
170. *Titanium and Burlwood Brooch*
171. *Black Titanium Cuff*
172. *Titanium Manchettes with diamonds and Tanzanite*
173. *Black Titanium Cuff with crystals*
174. *Multi-coloured Titanium bracelet*

IDH TITANIUM

GEMFIELDS

54 Jermyn Street

London, SW1Y 6LX

UK

Tel +44 (0)20 7518 3400

gemfields.co.uk

Image Description

195. *Deep Green Emerald*
196. *Givewell Chikuwe, Kagem boiler maker, 60. From the Chiparamba Village, Chipata District, Eastern Province. An employee of the mine for six years, Givewell, a widower, has eight children, and enjoys football and running.*
197. *Deep Purple Amethyst*
198. *Deep Green Emerald*
199. *Jewels created by Munnu Kasliwal for Gemfield's Emeralds for Elephants Campaign*
200. *The magnificent Zambian landscape, which Gemfields works hard to preserve.*

GEMFIELDS

HERITAGE

Image Description

192. *Gold and Plique-à-jour Enamel Morning Glory*
193. *Pendant Brooch (Marcus &Co New York) circa 1900 Peridot and Diamond Suite (by Siegelson , New York)*
194. *Art Moderne Blue Chalcedony Sapphire and Diamond Suite (Suzanne Belperron) Paris circa 1935,*

JAR

8 King Street,

St James's

London, SW1Y 6QT

UK

Tel +44 (0)20 7839 9060

Image Description

1. *Poppy Flower Brooch of Diamonds, Pink and Green Tourmaline (JAR) 1982.*
2. *Ruby and Diamond Camelia Flower (JAR) 2003*

CHRISTIE'S

JJBUCKAR

I'TL +1 416 364 7989
N. AMERICA +1 888 684 7775
Jacob@J.J.Buckar.com

IMAGE DESCRIPTION

48. *Golden Dream Earring*
49. *Topaz Eternal Tears Earrings*
50. *Zircon Celeste Ring*
51. *Aqua Lily Drop Earrings*
52. *Peruvian Wild Flower Brooch*
53. *Rose Quartz Star fish Ring and Brooch*
54. *Ocean Dream Brooch*
55. *Princess Locket Brooch*
56. *Wild Flower Necklace*

JJBuckar

LENA SKLYUT

NEW YORK
USA
TEL +1 212 380 3609
info@lenasklyut.com

IMAGE DESCRIPTION

175. *Double Snake Ruby Ring*
176. *Couture Spider's Web Set*

LEVIEV

KLG JEWELRY UK LTD.
31 OLD BOND STREET, MAYFAIR,
LONDON, W1S 4QH
UK
TEL +44(0)20 7493 3333

IMAGE DESCRIPTION

57. *Fancy Vivid Orange heart shaped diamond with multi colour diamonds surround*
58. *Pear shaped Fancy Intense Pink diamonds drop Earrings with pear shaped D-Flawless diamond tops.*
59. *Fancy Blue diamond Ring with pear shaped white diamonds surround.*
60. *Blue and pink diamonds Cat Brooch*
61. *Pear shaped Fancy Pink Flawless diamond and D-Flawless diamond Crossover Ring.*
62. *Fancy Intense Yellow and white diamonds set Necklace.*

LEVIEV
EXTRAORDINARY DIAMONDS

LORENZ BÄUMER

4 PLACE VENDÔME
PARIS, 75001
FRANCE
TEL +33 1 42 86 51 11
FAX +33 1 42 86 99 44

IMAGE DESCRIPTION

118. *Artichaut Ring*
119. *Pastilles Ring*

LORENZ BÄUMER
PARIS

MARGHERITA BURGENER

VIA TORTRINO 17/A
15048 VALENZA (AL), ITALY
(+39) 348 697 2568

IMAGE DESCRIPTION

63. *Aquamarine, Titanium and Diamond Earrings*
64. *Ramage In Rosa*
65. *Amethyst, Diamond and Rose Quartz Ring*
66. *Titanium, Morganite and Diamond Cuff*
67. *Into the Blue Ring*
68. *Monsieur Cufflinks*

MARGHERITA BURGENER

MICHAEL YOUSSOUFIAN LTD.

#C-D 10FL., KIMELY COMM BLDG.
142-146 QUEENS ROAD CENTRAL

HONG KONG

CHINA SAR

TEL +852 28689093

IMAGE DESCRIPTION

69. *Flower Ring: conch pearls, demantoids, diamonds*
70. *Emerald Earrings: emeralds, diamonds*
71. *Cross Pendant: amethysts, blue sapphires, diamonds*
72. *Ruby Earrings: rubies, sapphires, diamonds*
73. *Yellow Earrings: sapphires, diamonds*
74. *Emerald Ring: emeralds, diamonds*
75. *Fish Brooch: Peridots with green garnets & diamonds*
76. *Tourmalines Bracelet: Tourmalines, emeralds, blue sapphires, diamonds*
77. *Emerald Bracelet: emeralds*
78. *Conch Pearl Ring: conch pearls diamonds*
79. *Conch Pearl Brooch: conch shells diamonds*

M. Y.
Fine Jewellery

MIKIMOTO

179 NEW BOND STREET
LONDON, W1S 4RJ
UK
TEL +44(0)020 7399 9860

IMAGE DESCRIPTION

208. *Diamond Blooms Ring*
209. *Burning of 'inferior' pearls (Kokichi Mikimoto)*
210. *Pearl necklace*

MING

108 TALBOT ROAD
LONDON, W11 1JR
UK
TEL +44 (0)20 7243 6545
info@mingjewellery.com
MINGJEWELLERY.COM

IMAGE DESCRIPTION

96. *Octopi Earrings*
97. *Superman Ring*
98. *Lantern Earrings*
99. *Pagoda Ring*
100. *Paisley Earrings*
101. *Lake Palace Cuff*

NADA G

GOURAUD STREET, GEMMAYZEH
BEIRUT, P.O.BOX: 175-567
LEBANON
TEL +961 1 560591
NADAG.COM

IMAGE DESCRIPTION

177. *Matrix Ring*
178. *Aya Ring*

FINE JEWELRY

NICHOLAS VARNEY JEWELS

60 EAST 56TH STREET, 10TH FLOOR
NEW YORK, 10022
USA
TEL +1 212 223 1043
NICHOLASVARNEYJEWELS.COM

IMAGE DESCRIPTION

102. *Aquamarine and Diamond Horst Ring*
103. *Fire Opal and Natural Penn Shell Pearl Brick Bracelet*
104. *Orange Fire Opal Pilar Bracelet*
105. *Portonuovo Bangle*
106. *Paisley Earclips*
107. *Bird of Paradise Brooch*

NICHOLAS
VARNEY
JEWELS

OCTIUM

Unit M1-17, 360 Mall
South Surra, Zahra Area
Kuwait
Tel +965 25309 888
info@octiumjewelry.com
octiumjewely.com

Image Description

201. *Octium Tri Ring*
202. *The interior of the boutique designed by Jaime Hayon*
203. *5Octium Earrings*
204. *Fahad Al Hajiri and Alanood Al Sabah*
205. *Octium Single Ring*
206. *Piece by Vicente Gracia - represented in Octium Gallery*
207. *Piece by Shaun Leane - represented in Octium Gallery*

POONAM SONI

202-203, IInd Floor
Vatsala Niwas Chs Ltd
Plot No. 64-B, Linking Road
Santracuz (West)
Mumbai 400 054
India
Tel +91 982130513

Image Description

108. *'Gaudi' Bracelet with diamonds and Rubies*
109. *Antique pearl studded enamelled bracelet with diamonds, Rubies.*
110. *Carved Brown Tourmaline Butterfly Brooch with Diamonds*
111. *Blue Topaz Earrings with Diamonds and South Sea Pearls*
112. *Hornbill Brooch with Emeralds, Champagne and White Diamonds*
113. *Navrattan pendant with carved amethyst surround*
114. *Spiral beer quartz and diamond neckpiece*
115. *Falcon brooch cum lariat*

PRECIOUS METALS

Image Description

211. *Bracelet Araignée - (Lorenz Bäumer)*
212. *Heroes and Villains Rings: 'Churchill', 'Ghandi', 'Chairman Mao' (Theo Fennell)*
213. *Bracelet Diamonds, gold platinum (Buccellati)*
214. *Knight Dreams ladies Green Quartz Ring (Zoltan David)*
215. *High Jewellery ring (Bulgari)*
216. *Orchid Titanium Brooch (Francis Mertens)*
217. *Gold Damask Bangle (Nicholas Varney)*
218. *Victoria Ring (Lorenz Bäumer)*

SARAH HO

85 Mortimer Street
London, W1W 7SN
UK
Tel +44 (0)20 7436 6443
info@shojewellery.com
shojewellery.com

Image Description

179. *Aurora Necklace*
180. *Smoky Topaz Ring*

SHARON KHAZZAM STUDIO

42 Middle Neck Road
Great Neck
New York, 11021
USA
Tel +1 516 570 2663

Image Description

181. *Amethyst Tsavorite Big Ring*
182. *Mosaic Cuff Bracelet*

shawish
GENEVA

THEO FENNELL

Van Cleef & Arpels

YVES FREY DIAMONDS

VICENTE GRACIA

Calle La Paz nº 4 IZQ
Valencia, 46003
España
sergiokarrion@gmail.com
VICENTEGRACIAJOYAS.COM

IMAGE DESCRIPTION

128. *The Bejewelled Land*
129. *Once Upon a Time Necklace*
130. *Milky Way Ring*
131. *The Guardian's Treasure Ring*
132. *Big Green Ring*
133. *Mare Nostrum*

Vicente GRACIA
Joyas · Jewels

WALLACE CHAN INTERNATIONAL LIMITED

Hong Kong
Tel +852 2523 2788

IMAGE DESCRIPTION

150. *Circle of Light Earrings*
151. *Queen Mary Ring*
152. *Sonnet of Love Ring*
153. *Forever Dancing Brooch*
154. *Fish's Dream Brooch*
155. *Zen Brooch*

Wallace Chan

WENDY YUE

Rm 2105-2106, 21/F,
Peninsula Square 18 Sung
On Street
Hung Hom, Kowloon,
Hong Kong
Tel +852 2142 8188
info@wendyyue.com

IMAGE DESCRIPTION

134. *Carved Coral, sapphire and diamond ring*
135. *Carved Coral Rose and Swan Cuff*
136. *Carved Lavender Jade*
137. *Carved Jade and diamond Amphibian cuff*
138. *Rare Green South Sea Pearl Frog Ring*
139. *Opal, sapphire, diamond and pearl drop earrings*
140. *White Opal and Sapphire and diamond Flower Ring*
141. *African Safari Cuff*

WENDY YUE

YEWN

Shop 303, Level 3, The
Landmark,
15 Queen's Road Central,
Hong Kong
YEWN.COM

IMAGE DESCRIPTION

116. *Wish Fulfilling Lattice Ring*
117. *Cloisonné Peony Cuff*

YEWN
HERITAGE JEWELLER

ZOLTAN DAVID

Flagship Gallery-Hill
Country Galleria
12901 Hill Country Blvd.
Suite D-1-120
Bee Cave, TX 78738
Tel +1 512.372.8888
ZOLTANDAVID.COM

IMAGE DESCRIPTION

156. *Rubellite Ring*
157. *Hungarian Rhapsody Cognac Diamond Ring*
158. *African Promise pendant necklace*
159. *Couture Ring*
160. *Compass Star pendant necklace*
161. *Dusty Rose Pendant Necklace*
162. *Flowerfly Pendant Necklace*

ZOLTAN DAVID

ACKNOWLEDGMENTS

Credit and many thanks go to **Tamara Kaminsky** who brought her knowledge, writing and insight. Thanks go to Managing Director, **Christopher Rayner** and to **Will Sutton** for lending their continuous support and for their dedication day and night; **Nathalie Grainger** for overseeing Tamara's editorial and the project, dealing with clients and keeping the team calm, **Haydn Squibb** who was consistently efficient and who ensured that production went ahead smoothly and without any hiccups. **Giorgio Criscione** was exceptional as always. As the designer of the book he invested hours and hours of meticulous work on every last detail of the visual look perfecting the images so that they could literally shine on the page. The book could not look any more beautiful thanks to him. He received invaluable help from **Julian Luskin, Christopher Charalambous, Al Walker** and support from the entire Design Team. We owe a huge thank you to the lovely **Katy Parker** who helped us out with her invaluable time and talent when we most needed it. We are so grateful to you. A thank you must also go to **Alessandra**, our friendly printer in Italy for delivering such a beautiful product. Finally thank you to **Rebecca Tucker, Aaron Simpson, Ben Elliot** and **Paul Drummond** for their encouragement, belief and most importantly recognition of our work.

PHOTO CREDITS

Quintessentially Publishing Ltd.
29 Portland Place, London, W1B 1QB
Tel +44 (0)20 3073 6845
production@quintessentiallypublishing.com
www.quintessentiallypublishing.com

ISBN: 978-0-9569952-1-6